embracing
brilliance

© 2019 by Jennifer Norton ©2024 by The Good House
All Rights Reserved.
No part of this document may be reproduced, duplicated, or posted by electronic means or in print, and recording of this document is strictly prohibited.

embracing brilliance

*Contemplations on liberating
our True Nature*

jennifer norton
foreword by michael b. beckwith

The book is dedicated to my first best friends, my knightly companions and trusted confidants, my brothers, Chris and Brad, for teaching me courage.

Contents

Acknowledgments	9
Foreword	13
Introduction	17
1. Naming Our True Nature	21
2. A Talent for Life	63
3. Accessing Creative Genius	105
4. Our Physical Reality	133
5. Awareness of Circumstances	149
6. Living in Intention	191
7. And so, it is	219
8. The Courage to Surrender	247
9. Worldly Challenges	253
10. The Myth of Personality	269
11. Accepting the Calling	285
12. Embracing It All	299
My sincerest gratitude	305
Bibliography	309
About the Author	311

Acknowledgments

This written expression was inspired by all who've shed light on my true essence; thank you for reflecting the way Home. I want to acknowledge all those who have come before me, all who weave the golden thread of wisdom through our shared consciousness, and all who've chosen to stand in the light, come what may. With deep respect, I honor the Master Teachers with whom I have and continue to study, the Spiritual Mentors with whom I am blessed to pray, as well as the Life Artists with whom I have the privilege of practicing; my sincere gratitude to each individual who has in their own unique way contributed to the blossoming of this book.

The Sacred Divine in me bows to the Sacred Divine in you.

DISCLAIMER

The information provided isn't guaranteed to be scientific, medical, or even accurate; it's all opinion and for contemplative purposes only.

A portion of the proceeds from the sale of this book will be donated to charity.

Foreword

"We all have genius within, but not everyone is aware of it, and that awareness is what makes the difference. Mediocrity is self-inflicted, and genius is self-bestowed.

— Walter Russell

In a world that often emphasizes conformity over creativity, it's easy to lose sight of our brilliance. We're bombarded daily with messages that urge us to fit in, follow the crowd, and suppress our unique gifts in favor of the status quo. But what if we dared to challenge these limitations? What if we chose to embrace our brilliance instead of hiding it away?

This book, *Embracing Brilliance,* is a celebration of the Inherent Creativity and Genius that resides within each one of us. It is a call to action for those who have ever felt stifled or held back by the constraints of their own limiting self-beliefs and invites us to embody our life by brightly shining our light as the original masterpieces we are.

Jennifer Norton, an Agape Licensed Spiritual Practitioner whom I've known and watched over the years, knows the transformative power of embracing her own brilliance. Like many of us, she spent years doubting herself, questioning her abilities, and playing small to avoid standing out. But through her journey of self-discovery and acceptance, Jennifer eventually realized that her uniqueness was not something to feel ashamed about or hide but rather something to be acknowledged and celebrated!

Embracing Brilliance bids us to embark on a similar journey of self-awareness and recognition. Throughout the pages of this book, you will find practical insights, inspiring stories, and powerful yet playful exercises designed to help you tap into your creative potential and unleash your inner genius.

One of the key themes of this book is the idea that brilliance comes in many forms. It is not just about artistic talent or intellectual prowess; it is about embracing the full spectrum of who you are and expressing yourself authentically in the world. No matter what you do for a living, what roles you play in society, or how you identify yourself, there *is* brilliance within you waiting to be unleashed.

Another central concept explored in *Embracing Brilliance* is the importance of self-love and self-acceptance. Too often, we are our own harshest critics, unforgivingly holding ourselves to impossible standards and berating ourselves for our perceived flaws. But as Jennifer demonstrates, true brilliance actually *begins* with our ability to recognize and appreciate our worthiness *exactly as we are*.

Throughout this book, you'll discover practical activities for honoring and building confidence in your creative abilities. From affirmations to mindfulness practices, you'll learn how to quiet your inner critic and nurture your Inner Life Artist with ease and grace.

But perhaps the most important message within *Embracing Brilliance* is this: you are not alone on this journey. As you navigate the ins and outs of Life Artistry, you'll feel Jennifer cheering you on every step of the way. Whether you're nurturing your Innate Creativity, seeking guidance, or simply looking for understanding, you'll find support and encouragement within these pages and in all of the services Jennifer so lovingly provides.

So, dear reader, I urge you to dive into *Embracing Brilliance* with an open heart and mind. Let these words be like beams of light guiding you toward a deeper understanding of yourself and having a greater appreciation of the brilliance that lives within you. In Jennifer's care, you will embark on a glorious journey of Self-realization, Self-appreciation, and

Self-expression. The world is waiting for your brilliance—now it is time to embrace it!

Michael Bernard Beckwith *Founder & CEO, Agape International Spiritual Center.* Author, *Life Visioning* and *Spiritual Liberation* & Host, *Take Back Your Mind* Podcast

Introduction

"Inside you, there is an artist you don't know about."

— Rumi

Amidst a *Life Visioning*™ session typical in my Spiritual practice, a grander expression sought an outlet through me. Guided by my mentor, Reverend Michael Bernard Beckwith, via his *Life Visioning Process*™, inspiration was ignited. Despite feeling unprepared and unsure of my ability to do so, I heard a call to communicate what is undeniably mine to share with the world. This occurred several months after having received a (chronic kidney disease) diagnosis, which I chose to interpret as an invitation to reevaluate my life. Consequently, I left my position teaching acting and directing at a renowned film academy and redirected my attention back to my Spiritual wellness. While sitting with questions around my artistic expression, the suggestion of this manuscript emerged like a spark of Genius: a complete vision that presented itself to me, appointing me as its channel, yet leaving the how-to details mysteriously uncharted.

Within me, a new perspective was given permission to flourish as the words flowed through my fingertips and onto the page. In order to communicate what was blossoming in my consciousness, I had to embrace my own unique version of brilliance. What was being asked of me was an entirely new definition of myself as an innately creative being. As uncomfortable as it was, I had to close the gap between what I allowed myself to admit about myself and what Spirit was showing me about Life. It took every resource available to me to heal my disbelief. I called upon countless Master Teachers for support, some of whom you'll find quoted within these pages.

What came forth is the offspring of no less than generations of creative contemplations I am fortunate enough to have been exposed to over the course of my ongoing practices and studies. The suggestions contained within would not have come to fruition without the playful collaboration and generous contribution of hundreds of *Creative Geniuses*, for whom my appreciation is immeasurable. What arose was a profound awareness of the insights, gifts, and epiphanies I'd been carrying around through decades of studies and work-life as an artist, be it as a painter, actor, speaker, sculptor, photographer, director, storyteller, writer, educator, or Spiritual Practitioner.

I see this text as a bridge that connects my understanding of Fine Arts with my Spiritual awareness. *Embracing Brilliance* refers to the creative and imaginative capabilities that are inherent in each and every individual. A tribute to Life as Art, it recognizes the organic inclination found in all of Nature to express authentically and fully. Regardless of the manifestation, innate creativity is a fundamental aspect of our Essential Nature that seeks to communicate, interconnect, and explore the depths of our experiences.

The Life as Artistry perspective vibrates with curiosity, exuberance, and the call to express something unique and personal. It allows me to engage with the world and myself in a particular way, finding beauty and creativity in every aspect of Life. It enables within me a sense of fulfillment, joy, and self-discovery while serving as a powerful tool for self-expression, introspection, and potential catharsis.

Aware that my intellect often emphasizes practicality, this book also contains pragmatic methods, productive activities, and technical practices for the reader while insisting that nurturing and embracing our *Inner Artist* is crucial for our overall well-being. *Embracing Brilliance* is a collection of contemplations, exercises, and activities most anyone can apply in the exploration and empowerment of our True Creative Nature, just as I had to allow in order to bring forth this manuscript. Witnessing my life experience as an interactive creative Masterpiece allowed me to tap into my authentic, essential, soulful self, accessing a fount of inspiration, self-realization, and Spirit-recognition.

The *Life Artist* within may lie dormant or as yet undiscovered in some individuals, but it is never too late to awaken it. Any moment can be a rebirth, an uncovering of what has always existed within. Engaging in creative activities, exploring new mediums, seeking inspiration from different sources, and embracing a mindset of experimentation and curiosity can all help to liberate this already present Genius within us. The more we embody our unique brilliance, the more we enrich our lives and the lives of others, empowering us to realize our Divine inheritance even more profoundly. May this text serve as a contribution to our shared experience of self-awakening, Love nurturing, and Spiritual blossoming.

With Utmost Love,

Jennifer

Naming Our True Nature

"At the bottom, every man knows well enough that he is a unique being, only once on this earth; and by no extraordinary chance will such a marvelous, picturesque piece of diversity in unity as he is ever be put together a second time."

— Friedrich Nietzsche

Just like the omnipresent embrace of the Universe that surrounds me, cradles me, loves me, and is woven into the very fabric of my being, my creative potential is a boundless, radiant force. My capacity for revelation, manifestation, transformation, imagination, expansion, and co-creation is an infinite wellspring, ready to be tapped into whenever my heart desires. I revel in acknowledgment of the creative Spark of Life within us all.

From this moment onward, I recognize and honor the *Creative Genius* I truly, naturally am. Simply by being alive, I embody the immeasurable brilliance known as Creation. It has many names, (for example: Goddess, God, Source, Allah, Spirit, Jehovah, Divine Love-Intelligence, Brahman, Beloved, Mother-Father, Yahweh, Life, Creator, etc.) and It expresses Itself uniquely within, though, and as, each one of us.

ONE WHOLE LIVING ORGANISM

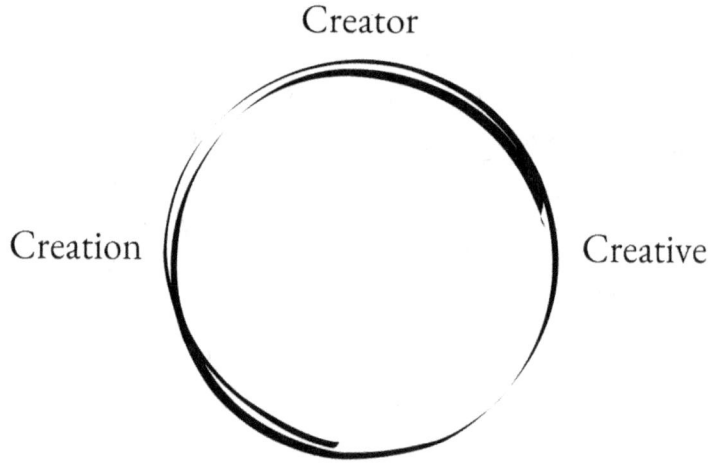

With my heart aglow, I celebrate the choice to consciously expand my awareness by delving into my inner wisdom and nurturing my authentic nature as an organically creative entity. There is a profound power that accompanies this universal responsibility I've willingly embodied as I chose to have a human experience. While creativity stands as the highest form of intelligence, society has yet to fully recognize this truth. Thus, I'd like to begin by acknowledging the creative impulse that brought you to this literature, uniting us in a tangible way, though we've always been connected. Welcome to the revelry of *Embracing Brilliance*!

> "Life is art. Art is life. I never separate it."
>
> — AI WEIWEI

When collaborating with a creative entity (i.e., any living being) on the intentional uncovering of our great creative nature, I've noticed that the simple act of acknowledging one's unique self-expression seems to uplift and enliven the individual, myself included. It never tires or wears me down to discuss just how sacred and cherished creative expression is to the human experience, often referred to simply as "self-expression."

When I was in primary school, quarterly and for six years, report card after report card arrived home with almost precisely the same phrasing, "Jennifer is an incredible asset to the classroom; I am delighted to have her as my student. HOWEVER, she does tend to talk too much." Following that, there would be some sort of request for my family to do something about my verbal gifts, perhaps squash them or at least lessen them enough to comfort whichever teacher. Not that my family didn't attempt to assist me and my educators in wrangling my expression to a tolerable level; I did in fact, grow up with two older brothers who were sure to encourage me to "stop talking so much" or to "hurry up and get to the point", according to their needs and wants. My parents, as well, made efforts to support my creative expression while also aiming to help me get along in the world. What they contributed to was the manifestation of a highly communicative person who is extremely aware of the impact and power of words, vibrations, sounds, and silences. As I navigated through life, I transformed my gift into a career as a passionate storyteller and communicator, breaking through limiting beliefs about my right to speak up to deeply connect with myself and others. Today, I carry within me the essence of those early report cards, cherishing the journey that transformed a talkative child into someone who now weaves words not only as a form of expression but as a tool to inspire and facilitate positive change in the world.

> *"Every child is an artist; the problem is staying an artist when you grow up"*
>
> — Pablo Picasso

Communication is one of our more developed tools for creative expression, be it verbal or nonverbal, be it visual or otherwise sensorial. One of the most impressive ways we interact and share the light of creation is through various forms of communication. From grunting to poetry, gesturing to ballet, hieroglyphics to cinema, heartbeat to music, communication as creative expression has accompanied us through the ages. To say that communication is essential to our Spiritual evolution and general well-being would be as much of an understatement as saying, "Art is essential for a healthy society." Self-expression through communicative interaction is Life-affirming, it allows the individual to be uplifted and to reflect while being reflected and a reflection.

LIFE MIRRORS LIFE

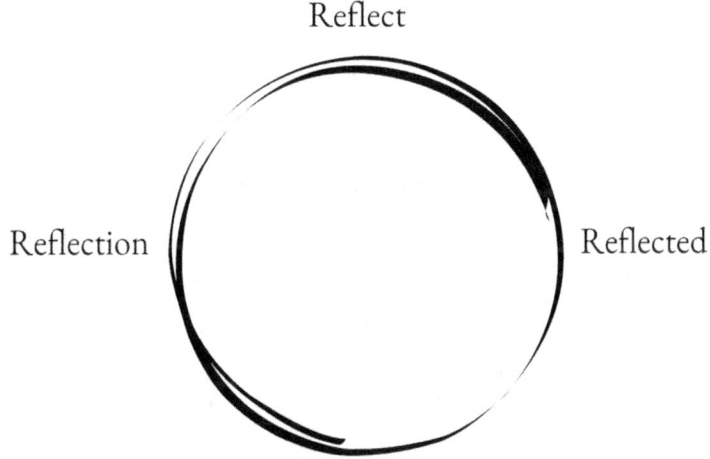

A sculptor may express through the medium of clay, a dancer employs the body as their creative medium, whereas a musician's medium is their instrument of choice. As a *Life Artist*, I communicate through the medium of relation, through interaction about self and others, as well as through being in relation with everything else in Existence. Each individual's contribution to the relationship is distinctive. Be it with myself, with fellow humans, with animals or with other forms of Nature, with animate or seemingly inanimate objects, and, inevitably, with Spirit, the quality of any relationship is found in the willingness I have to be present, open/available, loving, compassionate.

> "Relationship is the mirror in which we can see ourselves as we are. All life is a movement of relationship. There is no living thing on earth which is not related to something or other."
>
> — J. Krishnamurti

There has never been, and there will never be, anyone exactly like you or me; each individual is a unique and remarkable being. Our voice, our image, our stories, our creations, our awareness, our Life interpretations, and so much more are all unrepeatable original equations, distinctly ours. This fact invites us to fully admit and accept ourselves as marvelous expressions of perfectly original Geniality. I invite us to actively acknowledge the magnificence of our True Creative Essence, and perhaps to even put it to some serious positive usage. Just as we are each a unique incarnation of creative Source energy, our individual capacity for expressing the Spark of Life we all contain within is boundless.

If that feels like A LOT, well, that's because it is! No worries, dear *Life Artist*, so are you! And so am I. We are abundantly equipped with everything we need for this adventure into the particularly personal yet universal artistry for which each of us is made.

> *"Every artist was first an amateur."*
>
> — RALPH WALDO EMERSON

For a period of my life, I stumbled through a narrative of self-doubt and underestimation, not fully able to acknowledge my inherent brilliance. Seeing it in others was a practice I'd mastered when I was very young, while simultaneously learning that by pretending to be mediocre, others seemed to relax and be kinder to me. I noticed that people, consciously or not, wielded me as a mirror for their perceived shortcomings, fueling their habit of cruel self-comparisons, which I felt and which encouraged me to dim my Light. This was an expression of self-deprivation that I wore like an old, stinky cloak that doesn't fit and is not mine.

Years passed in this self-imposed shadow, where recognizing greatness in others felt natural, while acknowledging it in myself seemed an arduous task. This negation of self wore me out; it exhausted and oppressed me, stripping my Essence down until only a whisper of *excellence* remained. The relentless denial of my True Nature became unbearable, inevitably fertilizing a profound shift. It was up to me to tap into that whisper and turn the volume up again. With intentional Love, devotion, and disciplined self-reflection, I embarked on a journey to rediscover my Soulful Self, reconnecting with the Eternal Beauty within. Though the skill was learned, it is an ability we all possess; its authenticity now resonates organically as an integral part of my Sacred practice.

I have grown comfortable with *magnificence*, my own, and everyone else's, with the understanding that I'm not going to get very far on this adventure if I cap my possibilities or my imagination with limitations. What follows is a brief but potent exercise that guides my attention to the heart-center, the reservoir of Innate Intelligence within us all. With just a few moments of mindful practice, I can reconnect with this profound Source of wisdom, unlocking the transformative power it holds. Join me in exploring the essence of unconditional Love within.

Heart acknowledgement

Intentionally open your cognizance to include your physical senses.

Direct your attention to your sense of sight, noting that right now, this sense is engaged. Look around you until you find something you wouldn't normally focus on. Let your eyes rest on this object for a few moments... treat yourself to a sweet round of breath: inhaling and exhaling.

Guide your attention to your tactile sensations, continue breathing with ease as you feel your body, feel where your clothing comes in contact with your skin, feel your sit bones and thighs where you are seated...

Bring your awareness to your auditory faculty and listen now to your environment... while your full attention rests on listening, inhale and exhale gently.

Guide your attention to your olfactory sense and gain awareness of the scents in the air closest to you with every slow, deep inhalation and gentle, loving exhalation.

Inhale sweetly and slowly as you gently guide your attention to your gustatory awareness, taste the saliva in your mouth and the air on your breath as you exhale.

Breathing normally, become aware of the act of breathing; don't alter it or influence it; instead, appreciate it, notice its quality, allow it to be what it is, as it is.

Beyond hearing, seeing, tasting, touching or smelling, begin to sense what your heart is communicating to you, through you, at this very moment. Slowly move your hand to your heart-center and rest it there. Perhaps you can feel the warmth of the palm of your hand on your chest, or perhaps you can feel your heart beating loyally within the rib cage.

Now direct your awareness inwardly toward your beating heart... and inwardly to your heart energy-center, concentrated in your chest cavity and able to expand in any direction, several feet beyond your physical form.

There's only one heart-center exactly like yours, and it has information specifically for you contained within it.

Remember what you were born knowing: you must grow very still if you are to hear the heart speak. Allow a sense of peacefulness to overcome your entire being. You are listening, while resting gentle attention on your heart's expression. Curious and available to the secrets it has to share, you listen.

Beyond your mental reality, sense within that there is a deeper intelligence, a wisdom, and a connection that is beyond the intellect. Tap into your Inner Guidance System, your interior Creative Genius, your brilliant Intuition, by consciously connecting to your beautiful, generous, Infinite heart-center.

If possible, lift and roll your shoulders backward, intentionally opening your chest cavity, accessing a physical sense of your heart-center as it expands.

Allow your shoulders to rest, slightly back and down, sustaining a relaxed state of openness.

With your attention resting on your heart chamber in the center of your ribcage, with each exhalation, imagine enlarging that energy from the center outwardly beyond your physical body, out in every direction around you, above you, behind you, beneath you, an orb of energy expanding.

Perceive a field of your own unique heart-energy spreading outwardly, and realize this energy is inexhaustible.

See it as a colored light exuding from your center, your light, aglow, radiating, shining. The more you let it, the more it spreads, encircling you as it expands outwardly in every direction.

Observe how your body responds to you emanating your unique light... you may notice yourself in a state of receptivity, allowance, and stillness.

Listen. The heart speaks.

Hearts open, let's delve into profound acceptance as we embrace our individual innate artistry. By fostering availability, willingness, and curiosity, we unlock a realm of greatness beyond our current imagination, all the while nurturing our boundless capacity for understanding.

As a highly sensitive child, navigating the overwhelming currents of my heightened perceptions and sensations, often felt like sailing an uncharted sea. In those moments, my mom became a guiding light, offering a simple yet mighty catchphrase: "Baby steps," she'd say. Amidst the flood of sensations, intuitions, and observations, her calming words became a lifeline, encouraging me to find balance amid sensorial storms. "Baby steps," she whispered when emotions surged, and "take it one step at a time" when inspiration outpaced clarity. Through her gentle suggestions, I learned the Art of Piloting Life's Complexities, present moment by present moment.

> *"A journey of a thousand miles begins with a single step"*
>
> — Lao Tzu

We'll simply make a small movement towards an idea and include any new information that arrives so that taking small actions organically leads to ongoing revelations, improvisations, and creativity.

If, Dear Embodiment of Creative Genius, you find dis-ease with the ideas of either *creativity* (yours) or *genius* (again, your own), then this would be a great opportunity to carefully explore other words within this intended sense that might be more useful to you. The words we use influence us, and we, them, so we owe it to ourselves to be attentive and, in this case, select ones that tickle our hearts.

Other words for Creative... inventive, imaginative, innovative, experimental, original, artistic, expressive, inspired, visionary, resourceful.

Other words for Genius... brilliance, intelligence, ability, mastery, wisdom, expertise, artistry, capacity.

> "The secret of genius is to carry the spirit of the child into old age, which means never losing your enthusiasm."
>
> — ALDOUS HUXLEY

Taking Action

Subconscious and/or conscious fear may try to interfere with your explorations. Imagining endless, boundless potential may seem at first stupid/boring, frightening, or unnerving to some aspect of yourself. Discovering the great Infinite liberty found in the unknown, in not knowing, could seem scary or intimidating at first.

With that understanding, right now, you'll take a Baby Step.

One step... with the knowledge that your active participation in your conscious unfolding will increase your loving connectedness with all of life.

Trust in the awareness that even one small intentional movement towards your self-realization will create results, like a tossed stone splashing a tranquil body of water, rippling outwardly in immeasurable ways.

Show up today with the vitality of a child to incite playfulness.

Be available to your own creative expression in any form it takes.

Stand up today as a witness to all of Creation's continual unfolding Genius.

Take a step away from managing Genius in any way, today.

Right now, take one small step towards owning your greatness.

Allow the awareness of your own unique form of genius to be present.

Admit it, you're brilliant.

And, if so compelled, acknowledge the joy this truth brings, with a smile.

Enjoy being you, Life Artist!

Affecting our Actuality

As established, one of the most specific ways we express ourselves is through our relations. Be it the relation we have with ourselves, or with others, be it with persons, places, or things; the caliber of our relations is a reflection of how we interact with the world as we perceive it.

Unpacking that thought, I feel a natural inclination towards a curious exploration of the Arts of Communication, recognizing them as an important asset to my all-around wellness. "Arts" (plural) because there's no single right or wrong way to communicate; at least, I won't pretend to decide that within these contemplations. Let me, instead, entertain an adventure to see if I can arrive at a few solid options for the joy of my human experience. The path ahead might get a little uncomfortable, and I may hit some rough terrain, but I shall throw myself in whole-heartedly, sure that there is only one way to do anything, and that is *Fully*.

> *"The true sign of intelligence is not knowledge but imagination."*
>
> — Albert Einstein

Release any pressure you may feel towards having to "know" anything or come up with solutions or answers for anything in particular. We're not calling to service any part of the intellect that carries knowledge, so feel free to release those impulses. We are plugging into your Infinite imagination, or as Albert Einstein called it, your "True Intelligence."

Reflect on your infancy. Remember, you were an intuitive being before you had an intellect. You were a sensorial witness and observer, a natural participant before you were a words-forming, sentence-crafting thinker. You had understanding; you received and processed information while you instantaneously interacted and even responded, sans intellectualization.

Connection Reflection

Bring to your awareness a human relationship from any period of your life that you consider to be healthy, authentic, and truthful.

Reflect on this relationship, and without gripping for answers, be still and wait for your Inner Wisdom to respond to these contemplations:

What creates human communication in its most clear, most pure, most profound, state?

What occurs within me when I am tapped into my Core Essence, live in the moment, and consequently nurture connection within myself and with others?

How does compassionate relationship, realized

interconnection, and a true sense of unity occur? And can I will these things into being?

No one can control human connection; I can't force it into happening. I can, however, nurture my inherently heart-centered nature into being my primary, fundamental state of being. I can go inward and, in the stillness, get to know my True Essence, beyond what lies on the surface, beyond what I've been recognized for or as, beyond what I've valued about Life, or what I've said or believed to be true about myself, in the past. This inner movement is a vocation for me as a humane being, choosing to live in service of my innate and inherent Genius.

It is said that behind our human (finite) interpretation of this life experience is an energetic Omnipotent Omnipresence of Love, Infinitude, Beauty, Peace, Abundance, Purity, Joy, Creativity, Intelligence, and Benevolence. When I am able to observe Life as the Eternally and Infinitely Creative Reality that It is, while acknowledging my connection to this all-encompassing Love Life-Force... I birth the joyful and brilliant opportunity to be as One with All That Is. Liberated to be equally as surprisingly creative and endlessly inventive as the Universe Itself, and way beyond what I can currently conceive of or have ever seen.

Imagine the perfect project, one where we cannot go wrong; a surefire Masterpiece, where we will express unfathomable wonderfulness as we explore the unknown because we are not only capable, we are perfectly designed for the task at hand: to manifest a work of personal artistry, where everything that is conspires for our glory. Life, as our magnum opus, where our Creative Nature flourishes and expands because of the experiences we weave with Love and courage.

"We don't make mistakes, just happy little accidents."

— Bob Ross

Circular Communication

If actuality is energy, and playfulness is akin to imagination, let's use our energized imagination to contemplate: *an evening at the theater.* In your mind's eye, construct the theater of your desires... see the carpeting and wallpaper, the rows of seats, the curve of the balconies, see the footlights pointed upstage, the weight of the curtains, their color. Let's imagine we've treated ourselves to a beautiful evening out, a special event, a heart-gripping, life-changing, night of enjoyment. And having witnessed the most truthful, loving, amazing masterpiece of performance, see the curtain closing.

Let yourself feel an inner stirring of enthusiasm as if you *really* loved the entertainment.

See us in the audience. Join me on the balcony, stage right - that's your left if you're facing the stage - jumping to our feet, passionately applauding a show extremely well done, tears of appreciation streaming down our smiling cheeks. (*Yes, we liked it that much.*) And the actors, see their costumes and make-up, the lights changing as the curtain reopens, the swell of applause as they appear again to bow in gratitude for our participation. We instinctively clap in acknowledgment that we've been a part of, that we've just shared in, something special.

What I've always sensed in moments like this is that successful storytelling comes packaged in a beautiful, silent, triad agreement between the Writer, the Cast/Crew, and the Audience. From this perspective, we see a circular collaboration is essential for a lovely evening of entertainment, or in other words, for an event of clear, successful communication.

A CIRCLE OF COMMUNICATION

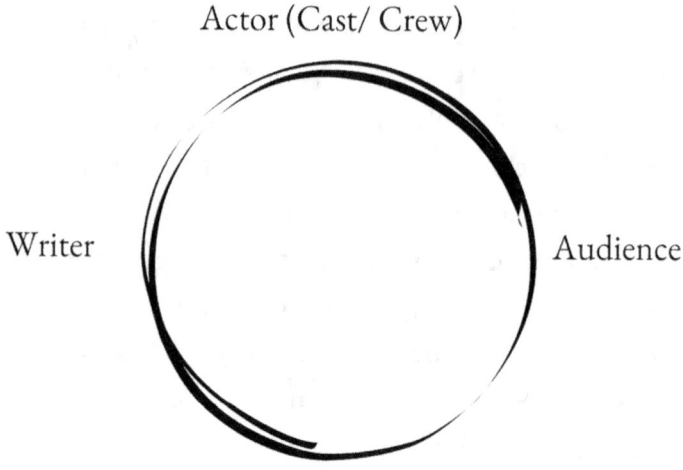

And we might even notice that when all three entities are at their best, utter brilliance and originality are more than probable. Because we've collaborated to create the proper conditions on these glorious occasions, there truly is space for Infinite possibility and continual revelation. We might even define these experiences as opportunities for the miraculous to take place.

> *"You must maintain a close communion with your true Center. Your creative power is not an act of will. It is, rather, an act of your willingness to believe."*
>
> — ERNEST HOLMES

Taking a moment to ground yourself, encourage a few slow and intentional breaths.

Invite your awareness to this ever-present here/now moment as you observe your body inhaling and exhaling.

With ease and allowance, release your will to achieve in exchange for a willingness to believe.

Here, you center yourself within, in close communion with your Inner Creative Essence.

Let's continue playing with this analogy by likening it to everyday Life. As we recall, we've got three key collaborative entities: the Writer, the Technicians/Artisans we know as the Cast and Crew (but for dynamics, let's focus on the Actors), and the Audience. In the place of the Writer, let's cast your intellect; in the role of the Actor, let's cast the rest of your entire Being. So, your body, your breath, and voice included, your emotions, your energies, your Inner Wisdom, and everything that makes you, you. And in the role of the Audience, let's cast everyone you care to interact with, be they an individual or a large group of people, your family or your team, the plants, and the animals; suffice to say: the

Life-forms with whom you wish to communicate successfully, intimately, truthfully.

A POSSIBLE COLLABORATION

Understandably, publicly speaking in front of a room full of others is, for some of us, a most terrifying and paralyzing thought. If you are experiencing any kind of fear response to this proposal, find comfort in the wisdom that one of the many marvelous qualities of our imagination is that our creative contemplations, our visions, and our intuitive explorations do no one, not even us, harm. Creative imagining is an aspect of ingenuity present in the early stages of expression, which can nurture manifestation. Allowing imagination to inform you as it stimulates brain circuitry is a healthy act of self-exploration. Feel the fear of imagining yourself onstage, then do it anyway; imagine. Set an intention to be available to perceive *beauty* and *goodness*. Channel your inner childlike curiosity and call on your playful heart's courage. Free your imagination, Infinitely Dear, Creative Genius, for the show must go on!

> *"I am indeed convinced that creative imagination is the only primordial phenomenon accessible to us, the real ground of the psyche, the only immediate reality."*
>
> — Carl Jung

See a technically bare stage, no set furniture or properties, just a simple black box, an intimate gathering place with you as the protagonist in a one-person-show. In this play, there is no fourth wall. You can make eye contact with anyone there. Envision yourself, the Actor, communicating through and with your Audience (representing all Life forms). See a fluid wave of heart-energy flowing from you through those with whom you are communicating; recognize that it is a circular exchange as you notice their energy is multiplied and returned to you, and vice versa, in an uninterrupted torus energy field.

Your intellect has written and continues to write in "real-time," the thoughts you have and the words you now speak. Meanwhile, you are consciously using your body, your voice, your face, your essence, your energy, and whatever tools you have to relay, reinforce, and clarify your communication.

You are fully listening; you are open, available, and receptive. Keen observation helps to inform your communication, influencing every intuitive decision you make.

Realizing that anything is possible within the confines of your story, you refrain from pre-planning your demonstrations, and instead, you're finding great *creative liberty* in not knowing what might happen next (within the confines of your story). Your receptivity is directed towards your Audience, for it is also through them that you will know if you've been successful in your inner embodiment and outward expression or not. And you are having the greatest time of your Life, being actively present, being fully available, responding freely and truthfully in the moment from a place of *completeness*, *balance*, and great *joy*!

From this contemplation, I've discovered willingness as an important component for this imagined level of creative availability. I notice that I am free to contemplate how willing I am to accept the great unknowns in Life. A feeling of gratitude arises organically that all three entities (Writer/Actor/Audience, or in this case, my intellect, my being, and All of Life with which I communicate) are willing to participate to whatever degree they are able. I find jubilation and perhaps even relief in the realization that the act of communicating is not a solo sport. We are not on Earth alone, with great reason, and we certainly are not meant to keep to ourselves, mastering the skills of relationship, interaction, and communication alone. A deeper sense of connectedness blossoms naturally in my awareness of Oneness, in my presence within relations, and in my willingness to be in intentional collaboration with all that I perceive.

CREATE A MOTTO for your unique version of Creative Genius

Gift yourself a slogan that encapsulates the change in awareness emerging within you.

Get a sense of your current heart's joy and put that into a few words right now and with very little thought; create a playful phrase that describes your ideal state of being, as it is, or as you would like it to be, when you are in contact with your inner Life Artist.

For example, could your motto be something like...

"Embodiment of Glitter-Light Love"

"Infinitely aware mega-joy Mastery"

"Fearless Interconnectedness Flow"

Or perhaps you choose to name your inner Life Artist...

"Galactic Creature of Cosmic Awesomeness"

"Liberty Colorific Speaks"

"Honor Sweet Fluency"

Use whatever words make you smile. Just have fun with it!

Write it down somewhere you will see it, and as you go through your day today, remind yourself of your motto.

Feel free to adapt it daily or at any given moment accordingly.

"The play was a great success, but the audience was a disaster."

— Oscar Wilde

Role Play

When looking at this apparent "night at the theater" example, I trust the analogy is easy to comprehend and perhaps even enjoyable to envision and imagine. Since we've established it in our mind's eye, let's examine this playful example from another perspective.

Let's recast the roles. This time, let's identify the collaborators in this way: in the role of the Writer, let's cast our beliefs; in the role of the Actors, we place our True Self as the creatively brilliant Protagonist (intellect included) alongside every other living creature in existence as the

Supporting Cast of Actors; and finally, in the role of the Audience, let's cast Quantum Energy, Higher Being, Creation, Organized Thought, God, Goddess, Source, Universe, Presence, Self, Soul, Brahma, Atman, Allah, Life, Infinite One, I AM Consciousness, Being, the Whole, Divine Mind, Beloved, Great Spirit, Yahweh, Creator, or whatever association we prefer for the many-named ineffable Power which sustains Existence, which is universally present and accessible to every living being.

Let's review:

Writer: our Belief System

Lead Actor: our True Self

Supporting Cast: all with whom we interact

Audience: The Infinite Source of Life Energy

A Circle of Communication

This production has an innate *balance* to it. The Writer is our beliefs; the Actors are all living Beings, all of Nature, and squeezed into the role of the Audience is Infinite Intelligence. Envision these three Life-Forces working together and sharing responsibilities, inclinations, and inspirations: to convey Love, to embody Light, to deepen our understanding of connectedness, to act from a place of *wholeness*, to behave from grounded intuition, to create and unfold and expand in *benevolence*, just as the Universe does; to realize our inherent *beauty*, our *creative infinitude*, our powerful, Loving essence.

In order for me to be all that I am called to be, within this creative collaboration, I acknowledge that a circle of shared intention and willingness is essential in this active version of reality, in everyday Life, and in every moment. I might even notice that when all three entities are at their best (affirming the absolute Perfection of this particular Audience, I'm looking at you, Writer and Actors), utter *brilliance* and *originality* are more than probable. On these glorious occasions of Conscious collaboration, there truly is space for Infinite possibility and continual, incessant realization: I might define these experiences as opportunities for the miraculous to take place.

Trusting the Audience, I bring the Writer, also known as Belief Systems, to the front and center of my awareness. I shine the compassionate *light* of my inner eye on the world playing out in my script. There is a collaborative agreement here: the Writer and Actors serve the Audience. I, as both, have a responsibility towards each aspect of my Being and towards that which those aspects serve. Consequently, almost instantaneously, my inner *wisdom* guides me to devote myself to those things which I have the capacity to change, respond to, influence, and to affect; as I organically refrain from vibrations, thoughts, actions and reactions, over the things upon which I cannot have an effect.

The current popular belief system might be chiming in now, asking us: Yes, but what *is* within my "control"? What is it that I am actually responsible for? What can I physically *do*? With respect for those highly conditioned requests, for it is not my intention to ignore anything that may come up, nor to judge it; instead, I observe and perceive as to comprehend what I can affect and contribute to, personally.

My friend, author Asli Eti, proposes a great starting point when she offers: "We are all writers, we all write our own Life Stories, we are in a constant state of inspiration and creation. Our thoughts and our beliefs about ourselves, as our own life story writers, provide us the most information, for it is the perspective from which we interpret ourselves and our lives. These are only opinions, not facts. All of our beliefs and thoughts about ourselves are formed early in life; some are positive and some are negative, and we embody those thoughts while writing our life story, integrating those beliefs, and making them our reality."

As your own personal story Writer, as its wordsmith and perspective-giver, what quality of text are you manufacturing?

And in which genre are you creating your life?

Is your story tragic, dramatic, a horror, a fantasy, a triple X?

Might it be an enlightened adventure script, a thrilling comedy narrative, a coming-of-age story, a love chronicle, a battle between good and evil tale, or a quest for discovery?

Is your storyline a fast-paced, egocentric roller-coaster? Is it a travel story of great courage and humble service?

Make a decision right now, not based on the past but based on right now.

A new project is starting; a new script is in the works: first and foremost, what is its genre?

Your options are as limited as you want them to be. I suggest you bravely go for the one(s) that make you laugh or smile, the one(s) that spark your imagination. If the options the world has constructed for you don't suit you, enjoy defining your own genre.

This is <u>your</u> story. Make it excellent!

"If you're going to have a story, have a big story, or none at all."

— Joseph Campbell

As the Writer of these ongoing, ever-evolving stories, I am responsible for creating a reality set in the present, within which my beloved Actors will play. As Writer, I dictate to the cast what their world is, for I literally create it. I give great, heart-expanding care to every single moment, movement, and utterance. Aware that subtext is created directly through intention, I consciously take on the job of being exceptionally intentional with my words. And with my silences.

I invest especially careful attention to my beloved Protagonist, well-aware that as the Lead Actor in my story, they are the physical representation of this experience, and they will lead the action by embodying their intentions fully. I intend to write with precision and clarity. I'm also aware of the *creative* connection between what I say, the words I use, my intentions, and the beliefs I have, which manifest the perceived reality my Protagonist experiences as the story unfolds. Thus, I will remain open to improvisation, giving myself the space to grow, learn, discover, explore, and to develop my gifts and other physical realities.

I consider the Audience, for it is That which I serve: the Love Intelligence aware that I Am. My expression is being witnessed; it is my contribution, my statement, my way of participating in this incarnation. I get to live, play, create, act out, embody, express, show, and use hundreds of other verbs in gratitude for this Beloved Consciousness. When tapping into this particular Audience... what occurs within me in reference to the "feeling" of this play we get to write? I have nothing but the blank page in front of me, Dear *Creative Genius*, so I take care to use every drop of ink benevolently. What else am I here to do, but embody the Magnificence of Life?

> *"All the world's a stage, and all the men and women merely players: they have their exits and their entrances; and one man in his time plays many parts, his acts being seven ages."*
>
> — WILLIAM SHAKESPEARE

As my life's Leading Actor, I get to put into action all of the *truth* and humanity I am capable of expressing, within the constructed circumstances, within the reality of the story my treasured Writer is constantly creating for me. Gracing the planet with my unique version of *geniality*, I come alive and serve a story with all that I am and beyond. I know myself. I've become an expert on human behavior. I've developed heightened skills for listening and observing. I know when to speak and when to allow for silence. I trust the text, confident it will come to me when I need it; I don't worry; I trust myself. I am available, always creating the space for inspiration to sprout; I'm ready to improvise and practice the first rule of improvisation, which is accepting all offers made. I have the capacity to tell the *Truth* of the Life form I am representing, in any given circumstance, beat by beat, without believing I am the character. I remain in the present moment only, acknowledging that there is no greater motivator, not even the text, than my intuition in relation with the Life-Forces (seen and unseen) surrounding me, in the now.

I get to admit what is within my "control," which certainly is not the behavior of the other Actors. Thus, I focus on my job, executing it to my fullest and best ability, every single take, or in this scenario, every single time the curtain rises. I am compassionate and enlivened. I *love* what I do and have been inspired to do it, not for self-centric reasons but for planetary and humanitarian reasons that go beyond the individual character I happen to be representing in any given story: this is bigger than me and I am an essential part of it. I get to bring to Life the world of my Writer with *love* and a great sense of responsibility, because I am sure to work with only the best, most trust-worthy, wordsmith.

As Writer and Actor, I serve the Audience with the utmost respect and gratitude, wise in understanding that It is here to be a part of my *creative* expression, and It wants me to succeed. It is cheering for me; It is along for the ride, friendly, and here to witness and to support my *unique* unfolding *genius*. The Audience *loves* me and gives me Its immeasurable heart, for more than anything, It is here to see Itself in me, to see the *light* of reflection, because I, as Protagonist, mirror Its existence, just as It mirrors mine. The Omniscient Audience already knows everything; I'm not here to teach It anything, and yet It wants to experience Itself through me, as me.

Albert Einstein implied a specific perspective when he explained, "The most important decision we make is whether we believe we live in a friendly or hostile universe."

Arriving together at the question, I propose we agree that the Universe is indeed friendly.

Years ago, I was studying the Laws that govern the Universe and came across Benevolence as Law, which brought up some doubt and curiosity. Like most people, an underlying contemplation often swam around in the sea of my consciousness that went something like this, "If God is Good... then why is there war? How is it possible that children are ever harmed? Where is Goodness in all of this human suffering?" So, I took it to the cushion! I sat in meditation, listening in the stillness. Silently, I waited for illumination on the matter.

What arose was an awareness of the inherent *goodness* that lies just beyond my opinions about Life. I could see and feel the thread of *benevolence* weaving through the fabric of Existence. It wasn't a simplistic notion that everything is always *perfect* in a conventional sense, but rather a recognition of the greater purpose and *harmony* within the grand tapestry of Life.

In that moment, the revelation unfolded: a realization that Life, as a Benevolent Power, encompasses a vast spectrum of experiences, each contributing to the evolution of Consciousness. I understood that challenges and adversities are not indications of a malevolent Universe but rather golden opportunities for growth, transformation, expansion, and the expression of Eternality.

This awareness didn't erase the hardships or suffering in the world, but it provided a profound shift in perspective. It illuminated the understanding that *goodness* is a Universal Principle, not always immediately evident though present in the blossoming narrative of each individual Life. Were it not, none of Existence would be able to exist, because the Omnipotence that sustains Life would have collapsed upon Itself in Self-hatred, It would have destroyed Itself and everything within It. From that point forward, I embraced a deep *trust* in the Goodness of Life, even in the face of apparent adversity, recognizing that every thread, whether *light* or dark, contributes to the intricate *beauty* of Cosmic Design.

> "You cannot control what happens to you, but you can control your attitude toward what happens to you, and in that, you will be mastering change rather than allowing it to master you."
>
> — Sri Ram

Things I get to have some influence over:

My awareness in the present (Where I direct my attention)

My willingness

My mentality

My thoughts

My beliefs

My energy levels

My activities and actions

My self-love and self-acceptance

My love for what I do and be

My intentions

My behaviors

My choices

My perceptions

My availability towards gratitude

My relationship with awareness

My state of being

The body doesn't know the difference between lived and invented experience. Which means, if I believe that something has happened, or is true, the brain behaves as if it were true, or has happened. If I believe something is happening now, my brain will release the chemicals necessary to confront said experience, whether it is actually happening or not, whether it is true or not. Luckily, I have various senses to inform me about what I am experiencing within a perceived circumstance.

All of what I believe is based on perception. My loyalty to a specific version of a certain story is a choice and usually isn't based on much *truth* at all. Cognitive Behavioral Therapy is a technical approach to mindfulness that allows me interaction with the story I'm telling myself and a way of becoming aware of the chemical response that accompanies it. As an Infinitely *Creative* Being, I have the ability to tell my own story, to write my own Life. In fact, it's said that the entire point of our *creative* inheritance is the *free* expression of our individual *brilliance*. It is in our perceptions of Life that we can find great *creative* opportunities. I realize I live in a world of my creation (based on my position in Consciousness) and that the reflective Universe and I are in constant communication, exchanging information, insights, and intelligence through inner awareness.

This next activity is one I picked up in a stray acting class I took on a whim with a gentleman I couldn't name if you offered me anything in the world. In an attempt to not misname him, he shall remain anonymous; however, his teaching lives on within me even today. I am so grateful to share it with you, with the preface that the first time I tried this exercise, I felt a massive shift in my mental perceptions, which then allowed me to heal the sometimes-rocky relationship I'd had with my grandmother. She and I shared a lot of Love between us, and she had a tendency to be so extremely judgmental that I often found it rather painful to be near her. I invite you to play with this activity open-heartedly and non-judgmentally, with *loving* intention and *playful* curiosity.

> "The universe doesn't hear what you are saying, it feels the vibration you are offering."
>
> — Abraham Hicks

Choose Your Version

Shifting perceptions is a creative way to experiment with possibilities, feeling tones, and perspectives. It allows us to playfully explore forgiveness, self-liberation and self-empowerment.

I suggest you enjoy this as a spoken activity; however, you may choose to explore it in writing. Perhaps you'd be willing to playfully experiment with both practices (verbal and written).

Bring into your awareness a relationship that needs improving, a relationship that isn't as great as it could be.

Bring to mind the person in that relationship whom

you believe misunderstands you or with whom you share a miscommunication.

Turn on your video camera and press record, or get your pen and paper ready and go somewhere you can be alone so you can really get into it.

Get ready to tell the story about this relationship, preferably out loud and in your fullest voice... but (now here's the catch!): say/write the **exact opposite of what your brain is telling you to say/write.**

Go ahead, tell us all about it... how you see them and how they see you... what they feel about you... what they think about you... what you feel and think about them... what they did/do to you... your participation in it... whatever you want to tell us. Let loose.

Just make sure it is the *opposite version of the story* you usually tell yourself about this relationship. Consciously empower the Writer of your Life to tell a beautiful story.

If you think, "They are so rude," say out loud, "They are so very kind and polite to me especially," sans sarcasm. If it takes a few tries to express it this way, do it until you can speak/write without sarcasm. Find the fun in making things up that you have no proof of.

If you think, "We are not friends, we don't get along," say, "What wonderful friends we are! We're really trusting of one another."

And so on, in this way, throughout the entire story, Consciously liberating the Writer of your Life to tell a fun story.

At first, it isn't easy; your Writer may argue "facts" with you... but stick with it, insist! Find the words to express the opposite of what you've programmed your mind to remember and recite, usually thoughtlessly and by rote.

Reframe the story and feel the difference.

Approach this exercise playfully... by simply changing the words you use.

You are exploring other versions, even if you are convinced they aren't true, because you have the ability to imagine such things because you are gifted creatively.

You are rewriting it or retelling it and observing how your nervous system and your physical and energetic bodies respond to the new version of the story.

Open your parameters.

Be creative in your word choice. Reach for new ways to describe the most beautiful relationship ever.

Exaggerate, go "too far" and have fun!

The Creative Medium doesn't hear the words we say. It responds to the energetic frequencies we put into It. This is an opportunity to alter and play with our energetic field in the privacy of our own contemplations.

A Talent for Life

"I'm a skilled professional actor. Whether or not I've any talent is beside the point."

— MICHAEL CAINE

As Innately *Creative* Entities, we need not distract ourselves by fretting over our ability, another word for which is *talent*, a concept often discussed in the Arts. As an undergrad in the very competitive professional actor training program at Tisch School of the Arts, I certainly heard several teachers tout that talent, if it exists, is not within our influence; "either you have it or you don't," and if you don't, there's little you can do about it. We need not devote such binary limitations to our perception of giftedness, as the appreciation of art is not objective. If we chose to limit our options to either "A" talent exists or "B" it doesn't, then, let's trust that indeed, it *does*, and that we organically, innately, embody it. Talent is defined as a natural aptitude or skill; I add that talent is an aspect of self that can be developed. I've personally witnessed "talent" flourish through profound devotion to and exploration of a specific subject. Talents, skills, abilities, and even willingness can all be nurtured within us. Our *creative* gifts are not so cut and dry, black and white, yes or no. But again, IF we only see two options before us, my loving suggestion is that we always go with the affirmative.

No matter what others, or we, have said about our artistic abilities and *creative* talents, in this moment of *Infinite* possibilities, we are *free* to allow the seeds of a new idea, a new thought, to be planted, to perhaps even be nourished into taking root, growing into blossom, and producing fruits. Let's be willing to release any lingering habits we may have of underestimating our inherent creativity. An intentionally slow, deep round of breath, and it can be done.

> "The one thing that you have that nobody else has is you. Your voice, your mind, your story, your vision. So, write and draw and build and play and dance and live only as you can."
>
> — NEIL GAIMAN

I'm reminded of and inclined to share with you the greatest director and acting teacher I ever had, who was with me in my first years of struggle, hunger, and, yes, even desperation, fighting for my education while NYC raged around me. Scott Zigler taught me courage on stage; he taught me how to be fully present no matter the circumstances and to fearlessly embody the *Truth* of any given moment as purely and wholly as I could. Several of the insights shared in this book were seeded in his presence and through his guidance. Although I was only fortunate to study with him for two years, it was enough to observe that Creative Genius has a home in him, is his constant companion, and clearly is the impetus for his Existence. I am so grateful for his service to the Creative Spark within me, his profound *love* of teaching and his precision, his clarity, and his integrity when it came to teaching the ancient Art of Storytelling to young hearts in *love*, vulnerable, earnest, and open. He was *good* to me, strict with me, saw something in me, and invited me to honor myself.

How delightful it was to arrive at the end of our first semester of study to find that Scott was giving every one of us an "A" as our grade! Oh, how useful that was for my scholarships, as well as being proof of my validity as an actor. I couldn't believe my luck! As a man of *wisdom*, he refused to grade us, refused to assign us a judgment around our merit. "Art," he explained to us, "is subjective. It cannot be graded! It is either truthful or it is not! And who am I to decide what is an "A" type of expression, and what is a "C" or *whatever*, type of expression?!" He was actually asking us. "You'll all get A's," and let's see what they say about that!"

We loved his rebellion and quickly joined him in his crusade to let NYU know that we would NOT be graded!

"Art is the stored honey of the human soul."

— Theodore Dreiser

Perhaps needless to say, the "powers that be" caught on immediately, declaring it impossible for an entire acting studio, approximately 30 students, to all receive the highest possible grade from this one professor. This was a comment I perceived as a self-image issue the University was struggling with, for I knew at that point what the truth felt like, and anything less than that became transparently untruthful. My youthful tolerance for anything that rang of falsity was minimal. I was being liberated and empowered and had very little "talent" for managing all that *expression, love* and *creativity*.

At the end of my second semester with Scott, he sat us down again and explained he was "on watch" as the University was keeping an eye on his grades this time and demanded he not give everyone an "A." As if he were being forced to betray himself, he gently went on to invite us to be honest and to not give ourselves an "A" if we knew we hadn't done our best, if we'd skipped assignments, if we'd slacked off. He said he trusted us to tell the *truth* and to do so honorably. We had to grade ourselves.

My heart sank. Not only was I an "A" student, I was simultaneously a survivor, a people pleaser, a self-effacing, wounded, scared, doubtful, child. I sat and struggled with an ego that insisted I was most likely not worthy of an "A" grade while my heart cried out in objection. Loving self-evaluation for an artist, and for most people, is absolutely a learned skill set, for initially, it can feel like devastation, massacre, slaughter, as it usually kicks in as we perceive imperfection in our expression.

The act of deciphering Truthful expression from untruthful expression is what the painter is doing and feeling as they look at the canvas, analyzing what is being communicated. "Is this *True*?" Another way of saying it is, "Am I being honest?" And if the answer is anything other than a resounding yes, which it too rarely is, the selfhood of the one in the midst of creating is touched. We identify with what we create; we identify ourselves through and as what we bring into fruition by our actions. It is a gentle, yet keen awareness to recognize we are more than that which we create, as we pour our very essence into Creation just as Creation has poured Its very Essence into All of Life.

"It is the writer's job to make the play interesting. It is the actor's job to make the performance truthful."

— David Mamet

It was challenging to decipher the fine and subtle space between myself and what I express, to learn that I am so much more than anything that could be captured in a word, a poem, a story, or a frame, be it 2 or 3-dimensional, still or moving. For much of my childhood and adolescence, I used my creativity as a means of self-measuring, self-knowing, and self-reflection. If I even slightly detected anything less than sheer illumination in the eyes of the beholder, I would destroy my artwork.

My mother, while raising three children, working three part-time jobs, trying to keep herself mentally stable and the three of us alive, was brought to trial on a regular basis, placed in the position of the judge and asked to throw down a verdict on my latest sketch, painting or creation. And she'd show up, tired, sometimes curious, sometimes uninterested, sometimes alert, sometimes distracted and strained, doing her best; she'd sit or stand beside me, and she'd let me show her what I made. And this was *love*; this was her loving a daughter who struggled to believe she was lovable. I'd pass her the paper or the object, my every sense honed-in and laser-focused on her: from minute facial expressions to the subtle battering of lashes, from the slightest exhalation to a turning up or down of the tiny spot where her lips meet. I watched her as if she were my personal hostage, as would an individual whose entire self-worth was dependent on her approval. It was too much to ask of another, and inevitably, less than a handful of artworks survived my adolescence. Forget about *"Embracing Brilliance"*, I was strangling my

Inner Genius, torturing my Innate Artist, putting on trial, and convicting my own creative expression.

"To be an artist, you have to give up everything, including the desire to be a good artist."

— JASPER JOHNS

As I traveled through my years of Fine Arts education, the concept of artistic evaluation naturally arose, particularly during my time at the Maryland Institute, College of Art, which I attended right out of high school. Despite the implied intention of offering helpful evaluation, I found that what was labeled as "creative criticism" often manifested as judgment without a broader vision.

Every morning, in every one of the fine art studio classes, we'd unveil our assignments for open critique from our teachers and our peers. In contrast to the common intellectually dualistic approach of defining expression as either "good" or "bad," when I eventually became an educator, a decade later, I chose a different path, opting for enthusiastic appreciation over judgment. This internal adjustment freed me from having to nurture in my students or myself a hyper-critical and competitive mindset, allowing my aesthetic sensibilities to evolve. The transformation marked a shift from a perfectionist perspective to a more liberated, open, forgiving, and ultimately compassionate *creative* relationship with artistic expressions.

Recognizing the *beauty* of individual preferences, I understand their relevance in shaping our sense of self. In the 'creative criticism' context, my personal preferences took a backseat, and I practiced discussing what I observed rather than focusing on judgments about the artist's capabilities. This approach enabled me to take responsibility for the interpretations my senses derived, and my mind deciphered, fostering a more enriching and collaborative *creative* environment, internally and externally. In retrospect, it is easy to see the seeds being planted in my young adult mind and the long gestation that followed. At seventeen, I lacked the maturity to understand my rebellion as anything more than a response to what I perceived as small-mindedness.

> "It is wise to learn; it is God-like to create."
>
> — John Saxe

By the time I was at MICA, I'd been exploring the Fine Arts for about a decade already. Thus, it seemed my "higher" education path would lead to a degree in drawing or painting. Although I knew "real" Artists with way more "talent" than I seemed to embody, I had been recognized as having artistic tendencies, a certain ability level, or however it is that we discuss these things, so I went to art school and promptly lost all belief in myself, what little I had to begin with. More than once, I've been known to declare that the quickest way to stifle an artist is to send them to art school.

When I was a kid, my mother, wanting to give me everything, wanting to give me something to fill the void in my heart created in my dad's absence, would sign me up for this or that art class. She knew I loved it. She saw I needed it, though she didn't necessarily have the means to pay for it. And if she somehow did, we certainly didn't have the extra money for any of the art supplies. But that was never a reason not to go to class. She'd take me, I'd go, and with an old brush or a borrowed box of oils, I'd manage.

I recall entering a drool-worthy art supply shop with her one morning after she'd committed me to a course we couldn't afford. We wandered the shop with our list of "required supplies" for the class, me struggling to suppress the full-on flood of desire running through my veins, and she, I imagine, looking for one thing, anything, she could afford. "Pick the most important one" she turned to me smiling, pointing to the list, "out of all these supplies, which one would you say is the most essential?"

Well, gee, that's a good question. It is a watercolor class, so, in theory, a set of watercolors would probably be pretty important, I contemplated, speechless and unable to decide. "Paper?" I eventually suggested, attempting to be as mature and reasonable as I could be. At ten, twelve, even sixteen, it always seemed to work out. I'd participate as best I could, and my creations would be recognized as having some artistic value. And with that, a sense of self was formed: Jennifer, who has more expressive skills than her brothers, who have other interests. It was a start, the beginning of a selfhood, a way of being unique in my family, a mark on the page that was mine and mine alone. I agreed.

And then I went to University, with nothing but the clothes on my back. Forget books; I couldn't afford food, much less expensive brushes, and new tubes of paint, stretchers, and canvas. Each class had a list of "required supplies," and I had almost none of them. I worked at the art supplies shop, I had scholarships, I shared tools with friends, and I still wasn't able to provide for myself beyond the most basic of needs. I fell behind. I missed assignments. I found myself in an abusive (romantic) relationship, and everywhere I looked, all I saw and all I felt was failure. Teachers began to question my commitment, my seriousness, and my validity as an Artist. That's when I realized I had no talent; I didn't belong there, and I was no *good*; in fact, worse, I was a failure.

I left Art School furiously. And I broke up with my art, officially, creatively cursing all the way to NYU, destroyed yet still very much a survivor. My heart was so upset, I was so hurt, yet there was no opportunity to rest or heal. There was just more running, more guessing, more barely surviving. Things didn't get any easier in New York; in fact, they became much more challenging.

Looking back, my heart opens; all judgment and the walls of the prisons I held myself in have long dissolved. It took me two decades to pick up a brush again, and believe me when I tell you, it was cathartic. By then, I had left NYC and was living in Firenze, Italy, and I couldn't pretend anymore that I was okay without my childhood companion. Oh, how I had missed my old friend! Oh, the years of regret and loneliness; I couldn't remember, I didn't want to remember why we'd stopped our dance together. Finally, we were reunited, and in that moment, the wound in me, born in a period of great fear and struggle, could begin to heal.

Gratefully, I arrived at the understanding that I am and we are immeasurably *Creative*. I began to see my Life as my greatest expression, and I realized that there is no way to quantify what I am, what I serve, what I embody, what I express, what I give, and what I shine *light* on as a perfectly imperfect, yet valid, participant in this thing we call Life. I found forgiveness for my perceptions around my worthiness as a *Creative* Entity and as a person. I took the misplaced responsibility away from others and gifted it back to the only person that could actually affect my potentiality. Our ability to respond to whatever we perceive is one of the greatest Freedoms inherent in being *Conscious*, thinking, feeling, sensing, *creative*, Spiritual, Living Beings.

Had you told the version of me that quit art school that she would one day show her paintings in the birthplace of the Renaissance, I would have laughed in your face in total disbelief. But it happened, Dear Life Artist, and I lived to see the day! I had an exhibition. I hung a series of paintings for all to enjoy or not, and I gave myself the honor of expressing and sharing, come what may. My intention was realized the moment I allowed myself to participate in what was seeking emergence through me. The process of bringing eighteen canvases to Life, the actual journey towards the exhibit, was where the healing occurred. I had to surrender again and again to what was seeking expression through me, surrendering fear, old beliefs, lies about my worthiness, and the chains of doubt rattling the cage I had put myself in. Every brushstroke, a release; every completed canvas, a yielding to the Inner Genius who demanded to be set *free*. I am steeped in gratitude for the *creative* process, for it gives all that it requests.

Let it be known: expensive (or used) art supplies do not make the individual creative! Every one of us has a talent for Life, simply by the fact of being alive. We were born for this thing we're doing and being here! This is our gig, it's our show, and we belong here. We are not merely upright walking, thumbs possessing homo sapiens; we are incarnations of Immeasurable Intelligence who also have all that we need within us; our inherent *magnificence*, combined with our willingness to play, is a most powerful combination for Masterpiece realization.

"When you are willing and eager, the gods join in."

— AESCHYLUS

By the way, I gave myself an "A" that second semester at NYU, along with the following two semesters as well, as one of the first acts in my *Creative Life* of claiming what is rightfully mine. Scott taught me to take a stand... for art's sake, for my own sake, and for the sake of *integrity, balance, justice,* and Truth, because it matters.

The Art of Being Fully Present

The Art of Being Fully Present encompasses the ability to successfully navigate any given situation, being able to instantly register what is actually happening and then actively participating in the present moment instead of being attached to the circumstances or outcome of events.

> *"Be here now"*
>
> — Ram Das

Resting my widened awareness simultaneously within, on my intuition, on my sensual responses, even on my cognitive associations, as well as on the other Life forms with whom I'd like to interact or communicate, instead of having goal-related tunnel vision, enhances my potential connection, allowing it to be more essential than my personal agenda. Where I place my attention is where my Life-Force flows. When attention placement is practiced intentionally, often, and deeply, I strengthen my compassion, thus fostering a more profound awareness of the connections within myself and with the entirety of Existence.

Focusing solely on the end result can be detrimental for a Life Artist, because although we serve a vision when creating, our *creative* space exists only in the present moment. Around the turn of the century, I found myself Executive Producing a domestic indie film festival in NYC. My primary objective was the successful outcome of the festival, and I was focused on bringing this vision to fruition in the future. I had the competence to fulfill my responsibilities, a task I took with extreme seriousness, as was my professional tendency. However, it was brought to my attention that a specific colleague desired something different from me, something I felt I couldn't offer: acceptance of what I perceived as the mediocrity of performance and lack of commitment. In response, I overcompensated by becoming excessively practical, logical, and humorless. I shouldered the festival's burden and contributed to the success of numerous filmmakers while neglecting my own Inner Genius, which was far from enjoying the experience. In doing so, I deprived myself of the *joy* of creating, the sheer act of causing something to happen, which can only occur in the present, not when the outcome is achieved.

I cannot control others; I cannot control my emotions. It would be inhumane to expect specific behaviors from others or demand specific emotions from myself. Instead, I am better off understanding my highest intentions and fully embodying them in acceptance of whatever emotions may arise, regardless of whether they unfold as envisioned. This is part of what it means to be actively engaged in the ever-unfolding "now."

Active presence, intuition integration, and acting with intention all require practice; they are aptitudes, a *creative* skill-set innate to us all but often neglected or forgotten. Through habitual application of readily available technologies, coupled with childlike curiosity and heartfelt *joy*, these talents can become integral to our daily lives, evident in our every action. Our practical abilities will then work for us, our skills for living will flourish, and we will find ourselves liberated to simply *be*. For instance, if we have deeply explored and intentionally nurtured our Sacred Listening skills, we are *free* to direct our attention to what is happening in the moment, rather than getting caught up in deciphering words, intentions, unseen energies, tastes, smells, sounds, tactile sensations, and visions.

Being fully present, as natural as it may be, requires courage, insight, and willingness. Courage is needed to embrace Life without fixation on the outcome, insight to sense what is transpiring and how to authentically engage with it, and the willingness to venture beyond our comfort zone and relinquish what we believe to be *true*. This means going beyond our past experiences, beyond our ideas, beliefs, traditions, and even our identity, to boldly stand in the unknown, no matter how daunting it may seem.

> "Remember that there is only one important time, and it is Now. The present moment is the only time over which you have power."
>
> — Leo Tolstoy

As virtual technologies advance and we explore new ways to disconnect, the challenges of nurturing our sense of *connectedness* become increasingly daunting. Yet, the desire for genuine communication, filled with honesty, authenticity, intimacy, and transparency, remains stronger than ever. We yearn for communion, not only with others, but also within ourselves and the Natural world. We hunger for inspiration that transcends the superficial and touches the deep well of Universal Truths residing in our Spiritual hearts, revealing our inherent wonder.

> *"To be an artist is to believe in life."*
>
> — Henry Moore

The choice to be fully present and to practice mindful awareness is a powerful intention. The world is calling us to bring our True Selves into the spotlight of *Consciousness* now, encouraging us to embrace our Authentic Nature and share it with the world. We've been given the gift of this very moment, a *present* from the Source of Life to us. In our awareness of the Now and our willingness to embody it, interact in it, live, create, express in it, and be fully present in it, we get to weave our intentions through it.

When our thoughts, beliefs, and actions align harmoniously, we have the ability to co-create in Consciousness, embodying the emerging experience, which is always more *beautiful* than any ideal outcome we may imagine. On the flip side, when there's a disconnect among these three elements (our thoughts, beliefs, and actions), we introduce conflict into our lives. This internal discord can lead to what feels like confusion, a sense of disconnect, or even self-abandonment. It is as if we are caught up in a convincing illusion of a dispute, a battle between opposing forces or interests.

It is said that "conflict is essential for creativity," just as it is said that "suffering is necessary for growth.". It is a storytelling pillar that the "hero" must be provoked by an inciting incident, a conflict of interests, and a crisis that cannot be ignored to accept the "journey" that awaits. This allows perceived conflict to metamorphose into a Divinely orchestrated beckoning, the beginning of something new; a birth, if you will, that may be a little messy, painful even, but is not a call for self-denial or abandonment—quite the contrary. Thankfully, if you are reading these words, the odds are extremely high that you are unwilling to harm yourself for being what you are: an innately *Creative* Embodiment of sheer Brilliance. No less.

> *"Creativity comes from a conflict of ideas."*
>
> — DONATELLA VERSACE

As Innately *harmonious* Beings existing in an Orderly Consciousness, we need not fear the experience of imbalance. Contrast serves as a catalyst for growth, and conflict often signals the onset of imminent change. Instead of resisting or fearing these shifts, we can embrace them as internal requests for transformation. When we become aware of that inner tug, it's akin to receiving a grand invitation to embark on a personalized evolutionary journey. With an open heart and being rooted in the present, we can fully engage with the opportunities for expansion and transmutation that arise. By allowing ourselves to lean into the discomfort we associate with contrast and conflict, we create space for profound inner shifts and external transformations to unfold.

Gandhi's *wisdom* defines happiness as the state where our thoughts, words, and deeds are all in *perfect* alignment. It's a *beautiful harmony* that embraces the paradoxes of Life without letting them turn into outright conflicts. Inner *harmony* acknowledges the complexities of Existence but steadfastly refuses to be consumed by conflict.

As we align our thoughts, beliefs, and actions, we're not only summoning a more magnificent reality to emerge, we're also nurturing a profound sense of Inner *peace* and authenticity. It's a journey toward greater congruence and self-fulfillment, one that can lead to a Life of profound *loving* kindness, *creativity*, and *joy* for ourselves and those around us.

> "Happiness is when what you think, what you say, and what you do are in harmony."
>
> — MAHATMA MOHANDAS K. GANDHI

The HARMONY of HAPPINESS

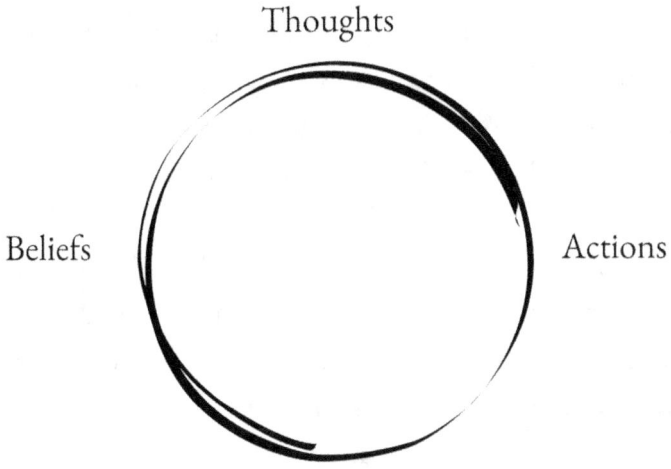

Within the realm of our mindset, *immeasurable potentiality* awaits emancipation. Our beliefs and expectations about what's possible reside in the confines of mindset. Think of your mindset as your own personal way of navigating the world, the set of beliefs that guide your actions and decisions. Now, here's the fun part: the realization that our mentality is the magical element that shapes the quality of the outcomes we encounter. It's like having a backstage, all-access pass to the most awesome event of your Life!

Picture this: Our Inner world is the Master Conductor, directing the orchestra of our outer reality. To paraphrase something I once heard Dr. Joe Dispenza say, our personality is like the scriptwriter of our own "personal reality" show. If there is *harmony* within, there will be *harmony* all around.

And here's a playful twist: Spirit blooms not by chance, but by choice. Fear disappears not by brute force, but by surrendering to the gentle embrace of awareness. So, as we embark on this exciting journey of mindset exploration, remember that we each have the *power* to be the captain of our own ship and the star of our own show. Let's welcome and accept our beliefs, nurture our awareness, and watch as our *Life* transforms into a unique-to-me adventure filled with our kind of playfulness and the confidence that comes with intentionally trusting in Life.

> *"Creativity is a natural extension of our enthusiasm."*
>
> — EARL NIGHTINGALE

Below is a unique guided meditative experience, a fusion of *wisdom* from two remarkable teachers, Eckhart Tolle and Dr. Reverend Michael Bernard Beckwith. This meditation is designed to be flexible, inviting cohesion between your thoughts, beliefs, and actions with *ease* and curiosity. This exercise is a portable toolkit for inner care, always at my fingertips. I offer you the *beauty* of its simplicity and the precision of its practicality. It's a meditation you can return to daily, allowing it to become a trusted companion on the path to greater self-awareness and inner *peace*.

Thoughts - Beliefs - Action: Meditation

Find yourself seated in a comfortable position, perhaps in a favorite chair, where you can sit without strain on your body. Some of you may already practice on a meditation cushion or yoga mat, but if you don't, have no worries. As long as you can sit/lay with your spine in alignment, allowing your breath to flow easily, you can do this exercise.

Take a few intentionally deep breaths now. Just let your body give itself over to whatever you are sitting on. Release your weight into the ground; let the Earth take that for you.

Bring your awareness to the present, to your body, your environment, and the "now" you find yourself in. Continue to breathe with intention, slightly longer and slower breaths.

You may choose to close your eyes or to focus your vision on a mark about 2-3 feet before you, lowering your softened gaze down front. Continue to intentionally breathe slowly and with ease.

If you find it difficult to concentrate, try directing your attention to your nostrils and tip of nose. As the air moves in and out of your lungs, passing through your nose, observe the quality of your breathing. Notice the sensation of air passing through your nostrils, becoming sensitive to the motion of inhalation and exhalation.

Continue breathing. Notice if any thoughts are coming to the surface. Without judging those thoughts, invite them to continue moving through you to their destination in the ether. Up and away. With this, you are simply practicing non-attachment to your intellectual processes; you are observing the movements of your mind without self-identifying with any particular thoughts, just as you observed the movement of breath through your nostrils.

As the thoughts (some seemingly demanding your attention, some lingering stealthily, and some releasing with ease) continue their migration, you continue your observation.

Ask yourself: *"Now, what will my next thought be?"* and eagerly await its arrival.

"What will my next thought be?" and wait for it. Look for the next thought continually.

Now, alternate your attention back to the nostrils, the air entering and exiting the body, as you remain alert and curious.

"Where will my next thought come from?" and listen, wait, sense, observe...

Now, *"I wonder what my next thought will be?"* Continue to await it silently.

Notice what happens.

Stay as closely focused on your breathing as possible, as if it were a dear childhood friend.

If it is morning, begin envisioning your upcoming day today; if it is evening, envision tomorrow. Let inspiration unfold and inform you. You are envisioning without guiding anything. Continue being aware of how you are breathing, and maintain the intention of breathing profoundly, slowly, and easily.

See yourself in your day as a continuous blossoming of miraculous outcomes. See your greatest, most beautiful, and highest self, tending to your every interaction with love and confidence.

Feel for yourself how you are when your Consciousness is elevated to vibrational states of generosity, joy, and gratitude. Allow those sensations to seep into your cells, feel your goodness, feel how immense your Spiritual heart truly is.

On your next inhalation, sustain the breath at the apex while you collect all of this energy in a bundle of metaphoric light within you, in your Core, where your Intuition lives.

When you are ready, fully charged, and electrified by your own potential, exhale deeply, spreading that light-tone all through your body, out from your heart to all around your environment. Light-energy radiating from your core, through you, and out in every direction, into the world around you.

Carry this sense of radiant confidence and heart connection with you throughout the day. And if you ever start feeling disconnected or stressed out, try returning your attention to that gorgeous nose of yours and the sweet breath of Life it ushers.

"Creativity is contagious, pass it on."

— ALBERT EINSTEIN

This next creative invitation is inspired by the *Illumined* Energy and sense of *balance* experienced in the previous meditation. Let's channel that energy into a tangible, *beautiful* expression. Let's dive in and let our *natural creativity* flow!

Thoughts - Beliefs - Action: Art Project

Express yourself to yourself! Based on your meditation and the images and energies that arise, create a collection of visual reminders and inspirations. Depending on your commitment to this project, it could take ten minutes to several days or weeks, so before you begin, consider in which medium you'd like to physicalize your realizations. Consider a journal page of cut-outs, a collage on larger paper, a collection of photos in the form of a vision board, a collection of digital images and pictures, or even mounting a slideshow or editing a video. You could go so far as to create an altar or draw/paint/sculpt what you envision. Whatever gets you excited and playful, do that!

This creation of yours will be a visual example, a physical demonstration based on a feeling dedicated to stimulating and supporting your heart's essence. Let this project be easy, fun, and visual: see your True Nature projected in these images. Don't worry yourself with how any of these realities will manifest themselves or how you will arrive at such glory. Instead, find images that reflect what is revealed to you when you are true to your innate brilliance.

When completed, put your project on display somewhere you can see it daily.

> *"Don't be an art critic, but paint, there lies salvation."*
>
> — Paul Cézanne

Tapping into Inner Wisdom

My beloved teacher and the founder of the Agape International Spiritual Center, Dr. Reverend Michael Bernard Beckwith, puts it eloquently as he writes, "When we stand, grounded in our *wisdom* that we are more than just a physical body, that everything is made up of energy, that our experience is a collection of vibrations, we recognize that our essence is way larger than we usually acknowledge it for being and that our Intuition doesn't live outside of us but rather, resides within our core."

One of our most invaluable treasures, an ageless asset that resides deep within us, is our Intuition, our Inner *Wisdom*. It's firmly rooted in our internal essence, an integral part of our Life Force. This inner compass is unwavering; as we learn its language, we see it never deceives us and never lets us down. Whenever we experience that Intuitive Nudge, whether or not we choose to acknowledge it, we are in direct communication with our innate Inner Guidance System.

> *"A good artist lets his intuition lead him wherever it wants."*
>
> — Lao-Tzu

Harnessing the *power* of our Intuition is simply another form of communication, a dialogue with our inherent *wisdom*. When our Intuition is finely attuned, we discern *Truth* by the way it resonates within us.

Occasionally, Intuition may be mistaken for its more impulsive counterpart, the "Gut Instinct." However, True Intuition transcends mere reactions. The fight-flight-freeze-fright-fawn response, stemming from our ego's instinct for self-preservation, is a basic survival mechanism. In contrast, Intuition operates on a different plane altogether. It goes beyond sensory input and intellectual analysis; it's the offspring of Universal Wisdom and our unique self-expression. It's an innate gift, entirely ours to embrace.

When we acknowledge, cultivate, and cherish our Intuition, it generously bestows its insights upon us. We develop a *loving* relationship with it, living each insight with gratitude for the *freedom* it imparts. If we invest close attention, we realize that it's our minds that can lead us astray, veering us off course and distorting our perception of reality. Although our minds are incredibly capable, they can sometimes misguide us. In contrast, our Intuition is a source of pure Intelligence, connecting us to the One Mind of Consciousness. While it may not always be easy to comprehend or decipher, our task is to observe it, trust it, and learn to listen to its whispers.

"Intuition is a spiritual faculty and does not explain, but simply points the way."

— Florence Scovel Shinn

Many individuals are unfamiliar with how to tap into their inner *wisdom*, let alone act upon it. Most folks are deeply rooted in their identity as intellectual beings. Yet, by embracing and honing our intuitive capabilities, we embark on a journey that leads us to profound understanding of our inner selves and a profound connection with the Infinite Wisdom of the Universe.

As an innately intuitive and highly sensitive, clairsentient child, I possessed the empathic ability to perceive and feel the psychological and emotional pain radiating from others. Thus, I would aim to guide a parent, usually my dad, the psychologist, towards helping them. However, my Intuitive Nature often went unappreciated by the adults in my life, including the strangers I obsessed over assisting who admitted no dis-ease. Perhaps we all found it inconvenient, distracting, or uncomfortable, which led me to suppress and doubt this precious gift, a pattern that many of us fall into.

There's this ever-so-subtle line that delineates what belongs to me energetically and what does not: what is mine because it comes from within me and what is not mine because it does not. It is so supple that one barely perceives it. If it hadn't occurred within my own physical being, I might never have noticed it. The endeavor of exploring and comprehending the fine distinction between perception and projection landed in my lap, so clearly "mine" to enjoy.

I don't believe my experience was unique, as the structures we've constructed, based on our understandings of Life, don't yet fully support a *harmonic balance* between what we perceive internally and what we project outwardly, nor do they support how very *creative* the whole thing is. From what individuals share with me, most of us have learned to ignore or distrust our *Innate Wisdom*, and so instead rely solely on our learned wisdom. Through good parenting, most of us learned to doubt our Inner Knower fairly young, as our intuitive curiosity regularly placed us in a position to hear the word/tonal quality of "No," often accompanied by a worried, or worse, face.

This mysterious ability to feel the suffering and the disharmony in those around me was misinterpreted by me as "attraction." I left home at seventeen and unintentionally dated a string of people who had been abused as children. It felt so natural to lean towards the wounded so that even when I'd have to duck a glass bottle thrown at my head or sustain a kick in my back, I'd participate, well-aware that the pain wasn't mine that I was feeling. In other words, whatever physical sensations I may have been experiencing, the actual pain began long before that. And it did not belong to me. I felt it, and it wasn't mine to process or heal or even to feel.

"You know the truth by the way it feels." - Anonymous

I was well aware of being in harm's way, but I allowed it anyway. I understood innately that what I was experiencing was very far from *Truth*, but I didn't know that I could delineate myself from that feeling inside of me that tugs and insists I turn towards someone who would exorcise their pain on me. I am not a punching bag just because I can feel when someone wants to (needs to) punch something.

It wasn't my Inner Knower asking me to stay and tolerate abuse; it was my beliefs. What I came to realize is that no one else sees the world through my eyes, nor can they feel the way my internal guidance system does; those experiences are uniquely mine. It's taken time, but I've learned to embrace and *trust* my intuition, regardless of whether I fully understand it or not.

An Inner Fire to make sense of what I so deeply felt has taught me the importance of listening to and obeying my Inner Wisdom. It's a valuable lesson that has empowered me to honor my Intuitive Aptitude and stay True to my own path. I nurtured the gifts of being blessed with profoundly empathic senses, perceptions, and projections by engaging in self-compassion.

> "Intuition is really a sudden immersion of the soul into the universal current of life."
>
> — PAULO COELHO

Befriending the Inner Knower that Knows

As we are willing to delve deep within ourselves and search for any negative associations we may hold towards Intuition, we might uncover a distortion of information buried in our beliefs. This misrepresentation often tells us that our Intuition brings discomfort or even pain. But this misunderstanding stems from the way our Core *Wisdom* communicates with us through felt physical sensation, what we label as stress, anxiety, worry, anger, doubt, or even indigestion. In truth, these sensations, feelings, and emotions are all information systems, yet they are easily misinterpreted, especially by our highly analytical mind. Instead of recognizing them as *productive* and *creative* tools, we tend to mistake them as destructive forces.

When our Intention is to learn the Art of Listening to our Core *Wisdom*, we learn to decipher the language of our Inner Essence in a way we can understand and follow. The guidance that emanates from within is to be trusted; we are safe to invest in the belief that we are trustworthy recipients of this *wisdom*. Shifting our self-identity from being Intellectual Entities to embracing our *boundless energy* as innately *Intuitive* and *Infinitely Creative* Beings requires conscious effort and discipline. This shift can be challenging, as it contradicts various ingrained beliefs and because the concept of Infinity often feels like an external occurrence, something that happens in the vast Cosmos rather than within our own embodiment of the all-encompassing Life Force.

However, surrendering to an Intelligence that transcends our limited mental capacity is a simple act, though not always an easy one. Yet, when we allow this surrender to occur Consciously, it immediately activates our Spiritual heart and awakens our Core *Wisdom* into service.

> "Surrender is the only technique for the inner being to become active."
>
> — OSHO

It's worth noting that the entirety of Nature is highly Intuitive, and many of us, in our role as human animals, have almost forgotten how to *trust* what we inherently know within. In *Truth*, we are so much more than human, so much more than what we've ever allowed ourselves to admit. One effective way to begin reconnecting with our True Nature is by keeping an 'Intuition Journal.' This journal becomes a valuable tool in nurturing and strengthening the channel of communication shared by our awareness and our Intuition, allowing our Inner Knower to flourish and guide us in alignment with the organic and *powerful* Wisdom of Nature.

INTUITION JOURNAL

Journaling, Dear Life Artist, is a healing practice that has a way of gently inviting my mind into an always *beneficial* conversation with a deeper, grander Intelligence. It's the combination of my very own cozy sanctuary, communing with a Trusted Companion, and going on an intimate adventure exploring my vibrational reality at any given point.

As I immerse myself in the world of journaling, I uncover epiphanies, I lovingly document my intentions, I release waves of emotions, I watch the intricate dance of my thought processes and belief systems, and I give voice to the inner contemplations seeking *light* and *loving*. As I write, I nurture the language of my Inner Genius, a treasure trove of insights and reflections.

I also use my journal to capture the mystical, sometimes whimsical adventures of my dreams, to note any inspirations that arise throughout my day, to write out prayers, and so much more.

Now, when it comes to starting a journal, I always make sure to choose a medium that suits my lifestyle and the intended contents of the journal. Whether it's the tactile delight of paper and pen or the convenience of digital note-taking, I let my heart guide the way. And I tend to lean toward the hand-written path. There's something magical in the connection between the eye that sees the hand that gracefully writes on the page. It's as if the Universe itself flows through the ink onto the page, making the journaling experience all the more *creative, expressive, unique,* and profound.

A CREATIVE TRINITY

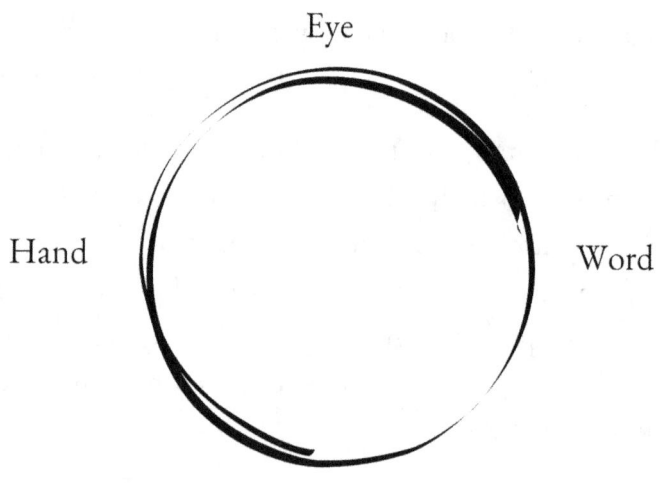

Journal Intuitively

Open your journal to a fresh page, and gather your writing utensils or whatever creative tools you've chosen to express your Intuition. Lay them out before you, like a painter preparing their supplies.

Now, take a moment to breathe. Inhale slowly and exhale gently.

Feel the presence of this beautiful Now, right where you are.

As you gaze at that blank page, recognize your intention: you are here to allow whatever wants to be expressed to flow freely.

Thus, with a welcoming heart, invite your Infinite Intelligence to join the party. Imagine your great Inner Genius, and extend It the warmest welcome, embracing It with kindness and complete acceptance.

Keep breathing, letting each breath fill your body with ease, and allowing whatever wants to surface to do so without restraint. There's no need for control, judgment, or decision-making here. Your only task is to document whatever wants expressing in your journal.

Here's a fun twist: if you're right-handed, put your writing utensil in your left hand, or vice versa. Don't overthink it. Just go with the flow. This works on a keyboard as well.

Begin typing or writing with your non-dominant hand. Let your Genius express Itself through your hand as if it were a vessel for your Inner Wisdom. It's all you, in full service to your creative flow.

As you write, listen closely, moving beyond the loud,

analytical, and critical voice. Instead, tune-in to the softer, gentler, heart-resounding voice within.

Be patient with yourself, especially if your Intuition has been ignored for a while. It's as if you're awakening an old friend who has been patiently awaiting you and has fallen asleep.

Keep breathing, keep writing, and if it helps, hum a song you loved as a child. Soon, you'll notice the power of your inner voice, eager and available to serve you!

Enjoy this unique relationship you're nurturing with your Intuition, for it holds immeasurable benefits and beauty. Through your willingness, may you rediscover a treasure within yourself that, with each journal entry, reveals more of the Brilliance that resides within you.

Journal with Intention

A powerful way to interact with our Intuition is to journal with precise intentions, such as:

- *to unearth insights from my subconscious mind*
- *to process life experiences*
- *to listen in trusting non-judgment*

- *to identify areas in my life where my compassion and forgiveness are expanding*
- *to find clarity and peace or balance*
- *to practice self-kindness and understanding*
- *to express what has yet to be revealed*
- *to declare freely what wisdom reveals*
- *to nurture my creative expression*
- *to uncover all that fuels feelings of gratitude*
- *to acknowledge all of the good within and around me*
- *to give voice to my Creative Genius*
- *to celebrate Divine synchronicities in action, what others call "coincidences"*
- *etc. (Add several of your own!)*

At any point in your day (or night), give yourself permission to not only hear your Inner Sage communicating with you, but to document it in your journal as well.

Rest your attention on what your Inner Wisdom reveals to you, staying aware of your insights and of observing the ways that situations manifest from within, not externally.

Being this intentional with your Intuition cannot help but expand your awareness, which invites *trust*, because it allows every part of you to now know that you are listening, present, and alert.

As you develop a trusting relationship with yourself through sacred listening without judgment, criticism, or blame, you soon witness the fruits of your compassionate loyalty. The idea is to create a safe environment for your True and Natural Genius to come out to play, thrive, and flourish.

"I invent nothing, I rediscover."

— Auguste Rodin

Intentional Intuition Journaling

Start simply, and let the words flow without censorship. Be exactly who you are when you journal. Never concern yourself with perfect grammar or spelling or handwriting, instead invite your organically creative inner genius to come out and play!

Here are a few starter options to get things going if you're new to this or want some inspiration:

- *I am grateful for... (This can be a daily practice for the rest of your life: Name three things every single day, and right now, name seven.)*
- *I am wondering about... (Limit this to a three-minute exercise with a timer, use it to clear out*

thoughts that are burying a deeper sense of calm and then move on.)
- *I feel... (This is a more profound dive within where we can name something that perhaps needs some form of our attention; don't censor and don't judge what comes out, just allow it to come.)*
- *I forgive myself for... (Here we go even deeper into our Inner Wisdom domain where beliefs and Core Truths converse; let it be whatever it is and forgive that too.)*
- *I love myself for... (Whatever this phrase conjures up may be of insight to you about your relationship with your Intuition.)*
- *I always listen to... (Another entrance into understanding the quality of your relationship with Intuition.)*
- *I trust... (This is a great starter conversation with our Intuition.)*
- *Self, I promise you... (Segue into a deeper dialogue with yourself.)*
- *Dear Sacred and Infinite Wisdom, I am open to receive your guidance on... (Channel Inspired Consciousness through your words; trust what conspires on paper as you tap into a wisdom that goes beyond experiential knowing.)*

Intuition Maturation

Exercise 1

Before you ingest your next beverage or foodstuff, take a moment to ask your Inner Knower for input.

Place your feet firmly on the floor, close to one another.

Take said food/drink into your hands, holding it mid-torso, near your solar plexus, a few inches in front of your body.

Now, close your eyes.

Your body will shift in one direction or another, and you may feel yourself tipping over, either forward or backward. Notice which direction you seem to be leaning.

If your body intuitively moves away from the thing in your hands, your Innate Intelligence does not want it.

If your body intuitively moves towards the object, your Innate Intelligence is fine with you ingesting it.

Open your eyes and decide: will you listen, or will you ignore your Intuition?

It's your choice, and it is always available to you.

Exercise 2

Arrange an opportunity to embark on a leisurely walk, one of those strolls where you won't feel pressure around time and when there's no specific place you need to be.

As you begin your excursion, take a moment to pause and turn your attention inward. You might even want to close your eyes, especially during the first few attempts at this exercise.

Ask your True Self, the Wisdom within you, to be your guide on this walk.

Trust that your Spiritual heart knows the way, even when your Conscious mind doesn't.

Imagine telling your mind, "Hey, you've worked really hard my whole Life; take a break from figuring everything out; I've got you!"

Intuition will gently nudge you in a certain direction, whispering where your Soul longs to wander. It's entirely up to you whether you choose to follow its lead or ignore it.

This simple act of surrender to your Inner Guidance System can turn an ordinary walk into a delightful journey of self-honor.

When you're ready, take that first step and see where your Intuitive Heart takes you. Happy wandering!

And when your walk is completed, remember to pause for a second of self-acknowledgement and express gratitude for yourself for this act of inner communion, trust, and guidance.

"Don't ask yourself what the world needs; ask yourself what makes you come alive. And then go and do that. Because what the world needs is people who have come alive."

— HOWARD THURMAN

Accessing Creative Genius

"Find a beautiful piece of art. If you fall in love with Van Gogh or Matisse or John Oliver Killens, or if you fall in love with the music of Coltrane, the music of Aretha Franklin, or the music of Chopin - find some beautiful art and admire it, and realize that that was created by human beings just like you, no more human, no less."

— Maya Angelou

Right here and right now, wherever you may be in the time and space continuum, you are an *Innately Creative Entity*, a *glorious* embodiment of pure *Geniality*. And although we are all part of One Living Organism and all made of the same stuff, we are also each one of us a *unique* expression of *Infinite* potential. As one with Nature, as an extension of what is *natural*, we share the same qualities and attributes;

we need look no further than our own yard, garden, or local park to uncover our *Inherent Magnificence*. We are creatures created by Creation. Thus, we are *free* to contemplate: How could we be anything other than Innately *Creative*?

Begin to ask your Inner Knower that knows:

- *What is my unique expression of Creative Genius?*
- *What is my specific way of representing Life?*

Contemplate with the intention of revealing the ways you might recognize, expand upon, and nourish your Innate *Creativity*. This awareness and your openness to its insights naturally nurtures your unique embodiment of Universal *Geniality*.

> *"If you hear a voice within you say, 'You cannot paint,' then by all means paint, and that voice will be silenced"*
>
> — VINCENT VAN GOGH

Criticism and analysis, at this point, are unnecessary; and no decisions have to be made right now. With sincere curiosity, refrain from judgment; no matter what surfaces, simply listen and observe. Ask these questions and enjoy what may arise, well-aware that judgment, no matter how well intended, distances and stifles your Inner Life Artist. Instead, let's tenderly welcome our True Nature to come into play, wise to the fact that judgment is the death of imagination, and that nothing blocks creativity faster than thoughtless criticism. Habitually harsh self-criticism is a learned skill that hampers our expressivity and one we would be well-served to release from duty as we benefit so very little from the practice. In the place of cultivating self-judgment, I invite the Consciousness of self-awareness. Let's recognize that the quality of the words we use influences our experience.

Often, for those who do not (yet) self-identify as innately expressive, innovative, or artistic, our associations with the concept of being a limitlessly *creative* Being lead us to turn to the Fine Arts for proof of this type of Genius. Our intention is not to compare ourselves to any other master, as we know said type of violence to be an instantaneous inspiration killer, and instead, we turn to the practice of non-judgmental observation with which to gain a deeper understanding of our own mastery. As we observe what we understand about artistry, we will be more able to recognize those qualities present in ourselves.

> *"Creativity is just connecting things. When you ask creative people how they did something, they feel a little guilty because they didn't really do it, they just saw something. It seemed obvious to them after a while."*
>
> — STEVE JOBS

The artist brings into form or manifests something born from an initial internal spark of feeling, from an idea, just as all of Creation does. The artist doesn't need any particular circumstances to express the *creative* impulse. However, when the environment is properly nourished to support any given expression, nothing can stop it from coming to fruition. The same is true in all aspects of Life. In every Masterpiece, the individual executing the artistry has a technique in relation to a medium, usually personalized, which they apply when working. One's technique is a collection of craft-related information and the knowledge of how to apply said acquired skills based on practice. The creator must know the medium and the tools available to them, which serve expression within the medium, and how to practically interact with them to bring their greatest *creative* inspiration to actualization. Likewise, (the medium of) Life offers us opportunities to discover what Genius is available to us and how we might put those gifts to use.

THE CREATIVE PROCESS

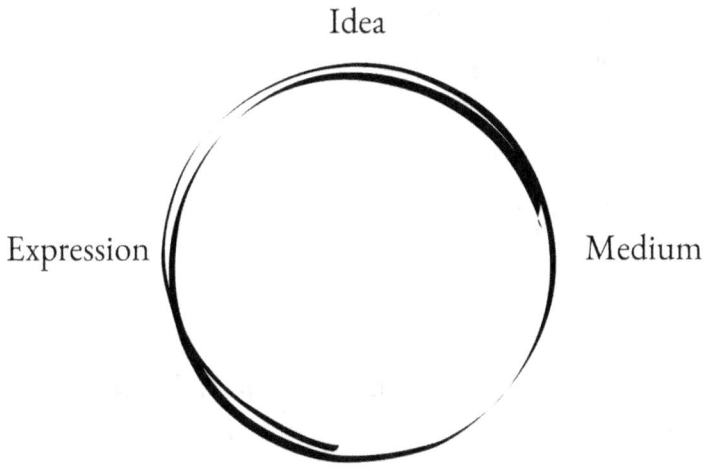

Truthful expression is a priority and a *natural* manifestation for the seasoned artist. Likewise, living truthfully wants an approach that includes Intuition and intention. Intuition is the inherent awareness of what is happening interiorly through our presence in the moment. Intention is how we are doing what we are doing (actually, what we are *being*), our energetic state, and the active process of working towards a possible outcome (not the actual outcome itself). We can only create in the present moment, where all possibility and all of Life exist.

The Art of Being Present deals with the Truth of the Now, as do the Life skills of successful communication, compassionate connection, *creative* communion, and caring collaboration. I want to recognize my inherent preparedness, as to empower my True Self to come and play, to improvise and discover, to fully flourish, in whatever given circumstances I may happen to find myself within, or perceive for myself and others.

> *"Acting is behaving truthfully under imaginary circumstances."*
>
> — SANFORD MEISNER

Our True Essence is not defined by what has happened to us or what circumstances we have been in or find ourselves in right now. To sharpen our awareness of the conditions around us that do not define us but do inform us, we can make a practice of identifying them. The given circumstances of any particular experience are fairly apparent to the naked eye; they are the environment and everything it provides (the material reality of the location, the season, temperature, clothing, ambient noise, etc.) in the present moment. Any physical qualities of the person/people/elements involved are also part of the given circumstances. Any physical qualities of our connection (distances, utensils and tools, even phones or devices, etc.) are also part of what is considered a circumstance in any given experience.

Limiting beliefs or engrained fears produce habitual and defensive behaviors, having us believe they are an integral part of the present moment when, in actuality, they are flashes from the past or projections of the future, which become dangerously destructive when we assume they are a given. In those moments, we bring to *light* the option to observe our memorized behaviors sans judgment, accessing the inspired choice to release them for something more honest, based on this very moment now. Improvisation takes place, our playful Life Artist appears, ready to participate, and we allow it.

In anticipation of what is manifesting, we can play at identifying any of the given circumstances within our current experience or situation that exists. We can mature our relationship with our *Interior Wisdom*, cultivating our Intuition. We can work on actively developing our intentions and expanding our options, safe in the knowledge that we are capable of realizing and experiencing any perception we wish to experience.

Improvisation occurs naturally thanks to our being open and available to inspiration in the present, and in executing those impulses fully from moment to moment, allowing for the unknown to take place and accepting all that is, based on the Life forms with whom we are interacting. It is by no means easy at first, and it's not meant to be.

> *"One is never afraid of the unknown; one is afraid of the known coming to an end."*
>
> — J. Krishnamurti

Remember, courage is essential to authenticity. If it were easy to be fully present, everyone would be just that: fully present. It is, however, innate in each of us; it is possible. In fact, we've all done it. At some point or another, we've all had an experience of such undeniable, eye-opening "realness" that it brought us swiftly to the present, where we remained authentically engaged, Divinely guided, and soundly aware, until the incident dissipated. Our inner critic returned, chattering away, judging and defining every little past detail, setting it in stone and fixing it to our mental reel: the stories of our Life, as it were, on repeat.

It is within our intrinsic capacities to be able to embody an active intention while observing so completely that we are able to instantaneously modify our behaviors based on Intuition. These are talents we can develop (and unleash) with ongoing awareness practices and technologies we can explore as tools for our enlivened expression. Technique won't equip us with the ability to be fully present, however, it is a utensil that when used in collaboration with our courage, insight and willingness, can liberate us to illuminate the essence of our Being, in any given circumstance.

One of the greatest opportunities in my Life I've had to apply these ideas is by the fact of marrying into an Italian family. My husband's parents and siblings, especially when I first entered their environment, were alarmingly jealous, surprisingly competitive, and palpably insecure. From our first meeting, I understood that none of their behaviors had anything to do with me personally and were all projections of their conditioned beliefs, limiting opinions, and learned fears. At the time, when I could have used an ally, they were unable to do much more than criticize, interrupt, and disregard me. It was a very painful form of communication: embracing my new extended family with my heart so full of Love, only to be treated as a threat and something to reject.

It wouldn't be productive or beneficial to list the ways I was treated, for it would only entail a significant investigation on my part into past experiences that I have forgiven and almost entirely forgotten. Suffice it to say, it distressed my sensibilities, and that anguish led to me allowing new possibilities. The felt "conflict" inspired profound reflection on what I was experiencing. Revelation ensued as I began to understand that although I behaved lovingly towards my new family members, my treatment of myself in that era had been nothing short of cruel. I was being called to create inner space for the immeasurable grief I was processing around events in my Life that they knew nothing of. The degradation I was being served on a hot platter was an indirect mirroring of how I was interacting with myself. And still, it was not personal, as intimate as it felt internally. It was simply the subconscious Creative Medium doing what it does, naturally.

What was being projected onto me had nothing to do with me; it was ignorance acting itself out, seeking a higher Consciousness through relationships. My perspective had everything to do with me, as I had found myself, once again, in a mindset of perceived failure and immeasurable loss.

Leaving New York, leaving my friends, my family, my career, all of my books and art supplies, and the Life I thought I'd have, while moving to a country where I didn't speak the language, had no friends, no family, no support, no work, was a rough transition I faced open-heartedly and courageously, and yet, a profound sense of sorrow accompanied this massive cultural change. I had to dig deep to uncover what was within my responsibilities and what was not. I was and always am in the midst of a grand invitation, a great opportunity, a lovingly orchestrated appointment, dependent only on my willingness to see it and interact with it.

As obvious as it seems now, it did not occur to me to apply my artistic abilities to these confusing relationships, and so it wasn't until I was at the end of my willingness to tolerate those dynamics that the paradigm was able to shift. There was only one way through this nightmare, and it was entirely up to me to bring about the change I was seeking. The techniques I share in this book are the same ones I applied to my relationships with myself and with various in-laws, who I now refer to as "in-loves," by the way. Setting an intention, and sticking with it no matter the circumstances, is a superpower. Embodying our True Nature, unapologetically and entirely, in our daily relationships and with ourselves requires the same courage it takes to put our heart on the stage, on the page, on the canvas.

"Creativity takes courage."

— HENRI MATISSE

One of the countless gifts I've received in my choice to live in Italy, adapting within the culture, learning the language, and loving the people, is an expanded familiarity of etymology. As a lexophile, I'm often delighted by the voyage a word can take from inception to modern usage. The word COURAGE has a delicious effect on my Being as I am reminded that its root is the Latin word for "heart." To have courage means to have heart, to act from your heart, to let your heart lead. Bravery, to me, implies potential danger and a call to face something that threatens my safety; meanwhile, courage, to me, hints at how to BE when facing the unknown, mystical, mysterious aspects of ourselves or so-called others. When I am courageous, I may feel fear, but I am in no danger, and I know it; I am merely in the midst of something new that is seeking expression, as well as my collaboration. I invite the Wisdom of the Heart to guide and inform my awareness in any circumstance, regardless of appearances, which, by the way, takes courage. I celebrate your choice to allow the same possibility within your daily life and am grateful to practice beside you.

"Life shrinks or expands in proportion to one's courage."

— ANAIS NIN

Our Essence

Love is our True Nature; Light is our True form, and Joy is our True vibration. Our unity with All of Life provides us with a direct line, an intimate connection, to what is authentically True about us. The essence of the Universe is our same essence. Based on what we understand, thus far, about the nature of the Consciousness that birthed us, is Its constant state of progression; It is not static, It is in fluid motion. It doesn't take anything whatsoever personally, for It has no identity; it merely *is*. The nature of Nature is pure *beauty*, pure *love*, pure *intelligence*, immeasurable *brilliance*, and infinite *creativity*; therefore, these qualities are ours, as well.

When it is difficult to find and feel the connection we share with All That Is, when our own *light* is dulled, or when we are seemingly unable to access any frequency of *wholeness*, we are, in those moments, identifying with falsities we've gathered along the way. No blame or fault is assigned to our collective species consciousness or our accumulated belief system residue. We redirect our energy by choosing to stop identifying with habitual fabrications that contradict our Innate Goodness.

Within our own Life, through our own experience, is where we can exercise, practice and express our greatest artistry. The quickest, most direct line to our essence and the world's remembrance of wholeness is through the vibrations of gratitude, *joy*, and *love*.

"Gratitude is wine for the soul. Go on, get drunk."

— Rumi

Natural Self Tuning

Allow your imagination to conjure up a most beautiful image of an awe-inspiring landscape of your preference.

If you find this to be a difficult task, find a photo or image of what you consider to be the most beautiful place on Earth.

Once the image is clear in your mind's eye...

Take your time and a few deep breaths to *envision* this place in nature. With your imagination, place your body there in that environment.

Dedicate a moment to taking it all in.

See where the sky meets the land.

Look there as you observe every color, sound, smell, and sensation within your nervous system as it responds to the glorious nature of life.

Let your appreciation flow through you for this perfect image. Feel these qualities to the best of your ability and allow them to impact your being right now.

On your next inhalation, fill your lungs to full capacity, and then at the apex of your breath, sustain it for a few seconds.

Then, deeply exhale, pushing the air out of your body with the elongated sound of "Ahhh....."

Take a few regular breaths, releasing all the information you've conjured up of colors, sounds, tastes, sensations, and even the vision of the location, allowing only the energetic quality to remain.

Simply feel the vibrational tone of what you are experiencing.

Breathe deeply, intentionally allowing this feeling to resonate throughout your entire being. It is a vibration, an energetic tone, a tuning fork, and it is contained within you.

That feeling, however we describe it, is precisely what you now may allow yourself to feel when you reflect upon your own awe-inspiring qualities and beautiful essence.

Everything alive is endowed with the *Creative* impulse to self-express, to embody *beauty* and *joy*, to *love* and be lovely.

Life is proof of Divine, Perfect, Benevolent Intelligence. All of Nature obeys the intuitive urge to live fully. As one with that which is *natural*, we, too, are invited to admit, obey, and celebrate the urge to live our individual lives to their fullest.

> *"As my suffering mounted, I soon realized that there were two ways in which I could respond to my situation: either to react with bitterness or seek to transform the suffering into a creative force. I decided to follow the latter course."*
>
> — Dr. Rev. Martin Luther King, Jr.

Observing our Innate Brilliance

The way we do everything we do, whether we are aware of doing something or not, is an opportunity to create. Our way of breathing, our smile, and our "me-ness" are just a few of the countless opportunities one has to be *expressive* in any given moment in Life. Consider how, in this very moment, you are creating your present experience; observe your posture, your breathing, your muscle tension, your self-awareness, any sense of connectedness you feel to your environment.

When we choose to embody awareness as an approach to Life, it can often and quickly bring us to *playful* and *fun* realizations. The ongoing opportunity to create is one such epiphany. The invitation to playfulness is undeniable, an offer that is ever present should one merely choose to participate. We only have to recognize the presence and the process, to become playmates with the Spirit of All That Is. Creativity is Life, as Life is Creation. Your Life, simply by its existence, is a remarkable and distinct expression. *Brilliance* is born into us all as part of our True Nature.

> *"You belong to the universe within which you live, you are one with the Creative Genius back of this vast array of ceaseless motion, this original flow of life."*
>
> — ERNEST HOLMES

Perhaps, like most of us, you've forgotten. Choose now to remember the miracle that is hidden within everything. The Genius of Life is contained within every Soul, in every expression of Life. Sometimes, we are aided in our self-empowerment through recalling a younger, more playful, less conditioned version of ourselves. Sometimes, it is easier to see the uniqueness of others before we can recognize it in ourselves. Sometimes, we are so full of our made-up selves that we hardly pay attention to the *immeasurable* Intelligence of everyone's nature, ours included.

In our daily lives, we travel, we work, we grab a bite to eat, we go to offices or classrooms, or stores for shopping, an infinite number of places where we encounter an infinite number of people, many of whom are strangers. Our thoughts drift from what we are doing, to a streaming internal commentary on everything around us. It's an unconscious, automatic behavior. Now the idea is to do it consciously, to practice being aware of our thoughts.

What follows is one of my favorite teaching tools when I work with actors and directors, for it invites the participant to not only open their perceptions and release habitual, unconscious bias, it also empowers the individual to experience a deeper appreciation for self and others. I learned this practice as a young actor, as it was my profession to become an expert of human behavior, a skill set I have nurtured for decades. Such an enriching exercise, I will often refer to it when I find myself in a public location with time on my hands. Perhaps you will carry it with you into your Life as I have, pulling it out for application whenever so inspired.

Creative Genius Everywhere

This activity is done in public, in a location where you can sit or stand or whatever you prefer, for an extended period of time. When first doing Creative Genius Everywhere, it is best to set aside an hour to ninety minutes for practice. Give yourself time to go deep into your observations. Then, once you're able to see the Presence of Genius everywhere, you won't need to set aside time to do it; you'll just do it naturally.

Take a moment to consider the suggestion. If need be, take an entire day to contemplate that every living being embodies Creative Genius. Each one of us carries our own entire Creative Genius within. Every human expression leads to the manifestation of Life. With the wisdom of a Life Artist, we can now envision ourselves, All of Life, and the whole world, as a creative experience. All of Creation is creative by nature.

In order to do the activity, intentionally go to a public location where you can sit for an hour, more or less undisturbed, where you won't see anyone you know. Bring your journal and a writing utensil with you.

Set an alarm for 60-90 minutes.

Direct your awareness to the present moment as you begin to consciously notice your breathing. Be sure you are positioned comfortably yet erect enough to breathe with ease.

Take in the environment as you inhale and exhale slowly through your nose. Relax your jaw, allow your vision to include the entire space, and widen it until you can see your own nose or cheekbones. Soften your eyes and release any tension around them.

Open your heart-center by imagining that with each inhalation your heart is expanding beyond your chest and body, and with each exhalation your heart is glowing brightly with a warm light that radiates three meters (or more) in all directions.

Without guiding your vision anywhere in particular, notice all of the Life that surrounds you. Include yourself in the observation.

Make no decisions, no judgements, no choices, as you allow your intuition to guide your eye. There is no need to rush, just observe with your whole self.

Watch yourself and listen to your thoughts.

What is true about you?

Look around you. Listen. Observe.

What is true about people?

Listen. Receive. Observe.

If so inspired, write what reveals itself.

While observing others, observe yourself and what feelings arise at any moment.

Write what you sense.

Stay present and keep your awareness sharp.

Be honest. Hold nothing back.

Write what you sense and feel and notice what occurs within you as you observe.

Allow this activity to be more about watching, listening, observing, and sensing than about having to document or record your experience.

Observe. Turn your Intuition on.

When writing, forget about spelling or grammar or quality of handwriting or sentence structure.

Watch the world around you as you listen to your inner voice.

Observe. Contemplate. Muse. Write.

Look at the people with loving-kindness.

Notice how you are breathing and what your mind is saying.

Observe others and yourself. Notice the aspects of humanity that interest you. What are you paying attention to?

Willingly notice, watch, look for, look at, see, feel, observe, witness, and testify to, the unique Brilliance, the Creative Genius in each and every Life form, yourself included.

How willing are you to decree the presence of Brilliance in the Life that you perceive?

Sense. Listen. Watch. Observe. Contemplate. Allow.

Include whatever comes up within you in your musings, and allow any judgments or old beliefs to surface. Observe them without having an opinion. Include yourself in everything you think about. Allow the truth of this moment to be part of your process.

Sense. Watch. Feel. Notice. Muse. When inspired, write what you are aware of.

Let it be as it is.

When your allotted time is up, consciously end the practice by closing your journal.

The point of this incredibly revealing observational activity is to heighten awareness, concentration, and, most of all, skills for non-judgmental observation.

Repeated application of it will allow access to deeper relaxation, stronger concentration, and more profound observations.

There isn't a right or wrong way to explore the Genius that is innate in everything and everyone.

Don't worry about reading what you wrote. The juice of this exercise is in the practice, not in the notetaking.

Gift yourself the playful freedom of curious investigation into this insightful exercise several times before you go back to read what you've written.

"Neither a lofty degree of intelligence nor imagination nor both together go to the making of genius. Love, love, love that is the soul of genius."

— Wolfgang Amadeus Mozart

Creative Genius Within

To remember and to liberate your True Nature, tap into what you already embody as a perfect incarnation of Immeasurable Brilliance. Life is for uncovering what you already know to be True, and to act on it. Experiencing your own unique version of Creative Geniality is your greatest endeavor, for it is through this act that Creation can know Itself as you.

Give yourself over to possibilities beyond your imagination. With playful curiosity and open availability, proclaim these empowering intentions.

Declare now, by saying out loud and with feeling:

I acknowledge my essence as an energy Being.

Observe. Notice. Invent nothing. Listen.

I accept my Natural Essence as a Creator.

Allow. Receive. Breathe.

I admit I am surrounded by loving support.

Observe. Notice. Invent nothing. Listen.

I allow my greatest Self to emerge.

Allow. Receive. Breathe.

I embrace the Innate Genius that is in all of Life.

Observe. Notice. Invent nothing. Listen.

I celebrate my own unique version of Creative Genius.

Allow. Receive. Breathe.

I am a unique expression of Love

Observe. Notice. Invent nothing. Listen. Allow. Receive. Breathe.

Throughout your day, remain aware; for as you have just declared powerful acknowledgments and have experienced a hint of the energy behind your Innate

Brilliance, Life will conspire to reflect and bring forth your unique, electromagnetic signature.

Upon repeating this exercise, apply various energetic frequencies, such as Enthusiasm, Joy, and Playfulness, to the speaking of the affirmative intentions to discover which serve your expansion and which shut you down; notice your willingness, your investment, your responses, to uncover blockages in belief, emotion, and energy. Play around with feeling tones to reveal which vibrational qualities produce beauty. Explore your relationship with yourself with the heart and the vision of a True Life Artist.

"Your Soul is your ultimate guidance system. You can think of your Soul as the compass, map, and destination, all in one."

— UNKNOWN

SELF-DECLARATION OF BEING

The fundamental theory of the Science of Psychology explains behavior through the analysis of thoughts and emotions. This explanation for how and why we do what we do allows for an exploration of our mental processes; it validates what we believe, asking us to inquire within and to recognize our thoughts and emotions as a source for self-knowing. Spiritual Science, Metaphysics, invites us to acknowledge that we have a mind, but are not our mind; just as we have thoughts and emotions, yet are not our thoughts nor our emotions, we are liberated to admit, finally, that we are so much more than what occurs in our skull. We are more than our behaviors, more than our actions could ever encapsulate.

Often, in therapeutic environments, individuals uncover a process that includes breaking away from unconscious behavior, igniting a beautiful new level of awareness in its place. Awakening to the relationship between our behaviors, thoughts, and emotions, we can observe our sensational responses, limited perspectives, and subjective opinions without acting on them. Our revelation invites an inner evolution of Consciousness in the form of self-awareness and self-knowing. For self-realization to occur, it isn't enough to have faith in or to believe in; we must actively cognize our True Essence and act from it.

"When we learn to love and understand ourselves and have this compassion for ourselves, then we can truly love and understand another person." –

— THICH NHAT HANH

What follows is one of the most challenging yet most rewarding assignments people new to the path of self-empowerment struggle with, self-Love in the form of Life-affirming declarations.

Imagine now, Infinite Good is blossoming from within you in the form of an energetic frequency. Acting as a wave, this vibrational tone wants to *become* you. It wants to manifest Itself from within you, as to know Itself as you. This "feeling tone" will have the essence of your original and unique Inner Greatness.

Observe, beyond your behaviors, your words, your beliefs, through your thoughts about yourself, beneath your opinions, even deeper than your feelings, abides your Inner Creative Genius.

Access the compassionate heart within you, and drop into tender awareness of your True Nature and the Essence of the Real you. Allow the energetic field of your deepest Core to reveal Itself to you.

Now finish these phrases, stating out loud three of your great qualities.

"I AM..."

"I AM..."

"I AM..."

If so inspired, begin a new section in your journal where you list all of your magnificent qualities. Dedicate at least three full (front and back) pages to this acknowledgment. Take your time to tend to this list on a daily basis for several weeks, if not longer. Don't feel rushed; don't embody a sense of need or of searching; simply allow your wondrousness to reveal Itself and be ready to take note as your unique brilliance surfaces!

"The arts are not a way to make a living. They are a very human way of making life more bearable. Practicing an art, no matter how well or badly, is a way to make your soul grow, for heaven's sake. Sing in the shower. Dance to the radio. Tell stories. Write a poem to a friend, even a lousy poem. Do it as well as you possibly can. You will get an enormous reward. You will have created something."

— KURT VONNEGUT

Our Physical Reality

> *"In art, the hand can never execute anything higher than the heart can imagine."*
>
> — Ralph Waldo Emerson

Breath

In exploring our intrinsic gifts, we quickly arrive at our relationship with our breath, which sustains us without any thought on our part and connects us to All of Life. Breathing is our Innate tool for accessing great focus and concentration, as well as states of profound relaxation and *tranquility*, *joy* and *bliss* included. Breath facilitates Life, and because All of Life is Creation, breath nurtures creativity.

It is easy to take breathing for granted without truly understanding its *power*. For me, it was a natural process I didn't pay much attention to until I was fortunate enough to study it in support of nurturing a voice and vocal presence that could "hit the back wall," as we say in theater. As I matured, encountering the challenges and stresses of life, I began to appreciate the calming influence of mindful breathing. I discovered that, in moments of worry or uncertainty, simply taking a few slow, deliberate breaths could be incredibly grounding and centering.

As I delved deeper into mindfulness practices, eventually becoming a Mindfulness Mentor, I was able to recognize breath as a bridge between the physical and the Spiritual, a vital connection to the ever-unfolding Now. It became a tool for anchoring my awareness and finding an immediate sense of *peace*, even in what one might call the "chaos" of daily life. My relationship with breath has evolved from something I took for granted, to a professional tool I chose to develop in support of my expression, to now, a profound source of connection and present-moment awareness. I see the breath as a reminder of the pure *power* we embody within ourselves, a hint to our Inherent Genius that we carry around with us and can instantly access at any time, anywhere.

Whatever situations or circumstances we may have found ourselves in, our breath has never abandoned us; breathing will always be available to us, wherever we are, until we cease to be in physical form. It is a great friend and True Ally, a beloved companion who deserves our acknowledgment and sincerest gratitude. A relationship with this organic process, this quintessential gift, brings *limitless* possibilities to those who recognize themselves as creatives, Spiritual practitioners, or high-level performers. It is worthy of our intentional exploration.

The world is jam-packed with information and technical guides on how one gets in touch with one's breath through practice. Ideally, you have a developed degree of awareness of the gifts contained in meditation and breath-work and their obvious, *endless* value in your life. If you are not yet equipped with a meditation and Conscious breathing practice of your own, you are fully capable of acquiring said skill-set.

As living organisms, we have the ability to ground ourselves in the present, recognizing our integrity with All That Is, as we apply basic breathing practices: for example, beginning with being aware of our breathing in any given circumstance, at any given time in space. Coming to that state of attention, we immediately access a connection to our heart, for when we notice how we are breathing (i.e., the *way* we are breathing, the *quality* of our breath) our heart-rate comes into our field of awareness. In that instant, we get to bring our attention to our heart-center, in gratitude.

When individuals begin to work with their breath as a means of self-care and deeper self-awareness, we can expect to experience a shift in our emotional state. As we tend to unconsciously breathe into the upper lung, a shallow breath is the norm; so that when our breathing drops into the more profound areas of the lower lung and abdomen, where perhaps we've rarely allowed our breath to reside, often an emotional break-through or energetic release can occur. A great suggestion I learned as I developed my breath-work practice is the insight that tears are just as valid of a release system as laughter. I had a vocal teacher who would tell us, "Don't you dare apologize for your tears! Do you apologize when you break out in laughter? No, you don't; you allow the laughter to move through your body because it is a form of energy release that is good for you. Crying is no different. When an emotion wants to release, let it happen, without judgment." Emotional expression is nothing to fear, for it is a gift, not something to control or manage at all, but rather, as with all gifts, something to nurture, honor, and enjoy. When emotions seek expression or release, it is simply an old energy wanting motion, wanting to move on, as opposed to getting stuck and manifesting dis-ease.

> *"Feelings come and go like clouds in a windy sky. Conscious breathing is my anchor."*
>
> — THICH NHAT HAHN

Count It Out: Exercising Breath

Breathe deeply and come to an awareness of the present moment within which you currently find yourself.

Become aware of your surroundings: listen beyond your immediate area, smell what surrounds you, sense what is happening within your own body and all around you and beyond and taste your mouth and the air all around you.

Realize you are grounded, wherever you are seated, standing, or reclining, and feel your feet, your rear end, your back, or whatever parts of your body are in contact with the ground beneath you.

See your connectedness to all living organisms, all connected to the Source of Life, all of Nature, and the Universe.

Continue breathing deeply and direct your focus to the slow inhalation and exhalation of your cherished Life Source.

Breathe in forgiveness; breathe out Love.

Allow a moment of gratitude for the breath that accompanies you always.

Begin to count the length of your breath: perhaps it is at a 4-count (4 seconds to inhale/4 seconds to exhale).

On the next inhalation, slow your breathing slightly, increasing the count by 2 (4 becomes 6, for example).

Continue at a sustained pace until you find your heart-rate has evened out.

Notice where the inhalation is arriving and settling in your body as it passes through to an exhalation. Release and loosen your stomach muscles, and let your breath drop into your belly area, deeper than your upper lung into your lower lung.

After a few breaths, increase the count by lengthening the breath by 2 again (a 6-count now becomes an 8-count).

Continue extending the breath, further slowing your beating heart.

Breathe in Love; breathe out forgiveness.

A sense of tranquility, of grounded wholeness, can now expand from within you.

Breathe in peace; breathe out ease.

You are here, right now, in the present moment, and all is well.

You are enough.

Your fullness allows you to operate from a place of wellness; you are overflowing with generosity, abundance, awareness, and gratitude.

If it were not for the relationship I established in my youth and nurtured through my adult life, with my breath work practice, even as a cigarette smoker for twenty-plus years, which wasn't smart, ideal, or even necessarily easy, I believe I wouldn't have had the inner support I needed to face and overcome the potentiality of a health crisis that showed up almost a decade ago.

A few (for lack of a better word) "symptoms" began to appear, grabbing my attention and forcing me to take action. For most of my life, I was accustomed to more or less ignoring my needs and living on as little care as possible. I am so thankful to declare these new physical events and appearances were precisely what I needed to allow a major shift in my perspective around self-care and self-honoring. Apparently, my biological parental unit, whom I do not know and who did not raise me, passed on a genetic "disease." All of my internal organs were affected. However, it is my kidneys that became the big concern. It took about a year and a half of a wide variety of tests before a physician was willing to give a name to what the exams revealed. During that period, one of my priorities was to sustain a state of *tranquility* and *trust* in Life that would allow me to face and willingly participate in said examinations, extractions, tests, and trials.

A sentient, empathic being, I'd often found it physically challenging to be in a hospital environment, whether I was the "patient" or not. Accompanying loved ones and family members to various appointments usually led to me losing consciousness and fainting, then vomiting upon awakening. So, you can imagine my concerns around subjecting myself and the array of technicians who would examine me to such a phenomenon on a regular basis. I knew I had to alter something within if I were to willingly cooperate with what was being asked of me.

Nothing has contributed to my well-being quite like Breath, and I would bet the same is true for you and us all. Co-creating with the Essence of Life, by embodying and moving from Its inherent qualities (which are vibrational energetic frequencies we all carry around within us and can access whenever we choose, sometimes with a bit of practice and certainly with conscious intention), I uncovered an Internal Presence that accompanied me through a period of great unknowns with courage, *tranquility,* and *grace.* Not once did I faint or vomit prior to, during, or after a visit to any medical facility. I actually began to enjoy the process, for it allowed me to embody Spiritual Truth and to deepen my already enlivened devotion to Sacred Practices, including but not limited to breath-work, meditation, ecclesiastical study, affirmative prayer, intuitive movement, creative expression, and intentional rest.

May we each learn to embody and act from our inherent Life Artistry, well-aware of our Holy Union with the Love intrinsic to Life. All this and more can be unlocked through our relationship with the Art of Breathing.

> *"To the mind that is still, the whole universe surrenders."*
>
> — LAO TZU

BODY

When we talk about tapping into our innate gifts, people speak of surrendering to a Force of Energy, often referred to as "being in the flow" or accessing an aspect of Nature we can also refer to as *limitless creativity*.

It is said that deep inner work allows access to the Source of Energy that is beyond human, something beyond what the artist, athlete, or practitioner could ever have imagined or created. Those who have invested experience in a *State of High Energetic Flow* will tell you it's an exquisite place to be. *Creation* and *fulfillment* come naturally, and although it isn't always comfortable, at no time do you feel under pressure or stress. We can describe it as *being* the process, in the present moment, and fully engaged, without any attachment to the outcome. Flow is available to all of us, accessible when we're able to step out of our intellect and inhabit our *entirety*.

Maintaining a supple body is essential for reliable access to and immediate use of it, just as nurturing a flexible mind is crucial for its ability to serve us as we require, on-demand, sans thought. Learning to listen to our physical body, to perceive and comprehend the messages and the wealth of information it provides us, allows for a deepening of our practice of living truthfully in the present. To access an availability to Energetic Expression or States of Flowing Fluidity with Creation, we remember to respect the body, for it is through our *existence* that we express Divine Intelligence. It is through manifestation that we are made in the likeness of Creation, even when we are immobile and believe we are not expressing anything. All action, even inaction, is *creative*. Being *creative* is unavoidable on Earth and in the third dimension.

> *"The big question is whether you are going to be able to say a hearty yes to your adventure."*
>
> — JOSEPH CAMPBELL

If we were to translate "flow" into something more specific, we could call it an ease of, or a familiarity with, an action. This interpretation connects us with the theory that repeated practice leads to flow. We might also refer to flow as an Energy Current with which we connect that allows us to fully surrender our *whole* selves to its *expression* or *fulfillment*. Sometimes, we just know something; other times, it takes us time to "learn" it through repetition of experience. Often, we find an easy connection to Source comes to us in some aspects of Life, whereas in others, not so much. We can, for example, get into the flow of walking, driving, or washing dishes. This is where we want to pay special attention, however, to our associations with comfort.

Just because we can do something sans thought doesn't necessarily mean we are in contact with Cosmic Inspiration. It can, at times, simply reflect our thoughtlessness, negating the spark of invention and intention, blocking the vivid observations that come with Conscious awareness. Being on "automatic" doesn't embody the same vital energy as being alert. Have you ever had the experience of, for example, walking or driving yourself home, and having no memory of the voyage as if from the moment you started the car's engine or took your first step towards your home, your entire body went into muscle-memory and delivered you where you were going, with no input on your part? We can call that "auto-pilot" and acknowledge that it happens often in our busy lives. In that state, we may feel separate from our Creative Genius, unintentionally acting from habit and not from awareness, and with that, we get to feel how it sits with us and whether or not we're willing to change that aspect of our experience, as we realize how much we long for connection when we are not present with ourselves.

Let's embrace this opportunity right now to explore and nurture our relationship with the Intelligence that guides, sustains, and maintains Life through our awareness of our internal vibrational essence. If your connection with the Source of All of Life had a voice, what one word would It say to you now? And how brightly would It shine if It were a Light Source? And if It had a vibration to It, what would that Energetic Frequency feel like within your body temple? Physically feel your connection to All That Is, was, and will ever be.

> "We are souls dressed up in sacred biochemical garments, and our bodies are the instruments through which our souls play their music."
>
> — Albert Einstein

The Finest Instrument in the World

Contemplating Einstein's suggestion about our bodies being "the instruments through which our Souls play their music", imagine yourself as a musical instrument of your choice. You can even invent one if you are so inclined!

As a Sacred Instrument, the notes you produce from deep within are sounds of Truth, Love, and Goodness.

In other words, Truth, Love, and Goodness express themselves through you in the form of vibrations.

You are a type of servant to the tones that you exude, for you don't think of making music; music *flows* through you.

The Spirit and sound of Truth, of Love, of Goodness, the Energy of Life emanate from you, using you, working through your very being, as your actual presence.

These are not your notes, or sounds, not your ideas or energy.

All you can do is allow it. Let it flow through you. Be it.

Now, as a loving instrument of brilliant creativity:

What are the vibrational tones you love to experience and exude?

Where do the highest (most excellent) vibrations resonate in your body?

Where do these various notes originate internally?

What qualities are embodied in these vibrations?

What sounds do they make?

How are you resonating?

What are you radiating?

Can you alter, influence, or change these Energy Vibrations by choice?

After you've listened to the Intelligence communicated through your body, take a few moments (or more) to find and express gratitude towards this portable temple you reside within.

Explore the sensations that come along with expressing gratefulness towards your physical being. A simple phrase that you can take with you and repeat as often as you like, and watch how it alters your experience, is an adaptation of beloved Thich Nhat Hanh's sacred "OUI/MERCI" practice.

Practice:

Gratitude. *Yes*. (Repeat 108 times)

Thank you. *Yes*. (Repeat 108 times)

Gratitude. *Please*. (Repeat 108 times)

Thank you. *Please*. (Repeat 108 times)

> *"If the only prayer you ever say in your entire life is 'Thank You', it will be enough."*
>
> — Meister Eckhart

If gratitude is difficult to access, that's all right; turn slightly towards an exploration of appreciation instead of gratitude; or, if still hitting a wall of resistance to appreciation, start with simple acknowledgment, then work your way up, energetically and at your own pace, to appreciation, then gratitude.

If you are an established gratitude practitioner, turn slightly towards the Art of Forgiveness for now. Self-forgiveness is a beautiful, compassionate practice to explore anytime. Some of us need to forgive our bodies for letting us down, some of us need to forgive (and dissolve) our harsh judgment and self-criticism practices, some of us need to forgive our Spiritual Self for taking physical form, and by doing so, take responsibility for our choice to be here now, alive in this Reality.

> *"Mindfulness is the awareness of what is going on in us and around us in the present moment. It requires stopping, looking deeply, and recognizing both the uniqueness of the moment and its connection to everything that has gone on before and will go on in the future."*
>
> — Thich Nhat Hanh

Awareness of Circumstances

"Don't think about making art; just get it done. Let everyone else decide if it's good or bad, whether they love it or hate it. While they are deciding, make even more art."

— Andy Warhol

Unthinking our way toward creative liberty

Thoughts formed as judgment color the Truth, taking us out of the present and away from Reality. Ideally and intentionally, we can get comfortable with releasing the habit of incessant intellectualization, arriving at what comes beyond thought, where great *freedom* can be revealed. Being fully present means letting go of our associations with past experiences, intellectual mentation, and memorized emotions, releasing habits, identifications, and our attachment to the known. *Freedom* from the ramblings of the finite mind, *liberation* from knowing or needing to know, release from having to identify or name what may or may not be occurring, allows a new awareness to come forth, an Energy and a *Creative* Vitality that is only recognizable when we are fully present, living in the Truth of the ever-unfolding Now.

My mind is an outlet through which Creative Intelligence seeks *fulfillment* and *expression*. Therefore, it's through the mind that I now playfully and willingly explore. I'll let my propensity for intellectualization serve my human need for some sense of security; I'll use this awesome tool known as my mind to observe "context."

When I first began experimenting with my *Innate Creative Powers*, I often found myself getting stuck in my thoughts, seemingly almost blocked and inhibited by my intellect. Thus arose the perfect opportunity to practice gifting myself but a moment of awareness to redirect that same mind toward a way of being that empowers me. I compassionately remember that I am not my thoughts nor my mind's minion; my intellect is an extraordinary asset in service of the Life Artist within me. Instantly, I access a state of being that is completely *integral*, where the observer and the observed are one and the same. The internal sense of separation between mind and Being ceases.

> "The intellect is a beautiful servant but a terrible master. Intellect is the power tool of our separateness. The intuitive, compassionate heart is the doorway to our unity."
>
> — RAM DASS

As I learned to be fully present in my most receptive state of openness, it became extremely beneficial to choose an intention for my state of being and my actions or activities. Creating a skill for arriving at a clear, non-biased awareness of any present moment is a useful ability to develop. In preparation for intention creation, I can craft a non-emotional, pragmatic reference with which to begin to identify any experience I'm currently perceiving. Keeping in mind the Universal Law that context creates perception and perception creates experience, I caringly proceed with focused attention.

Here is an example of a series of questions I ask myself that can, when properly applied, immediately clear perceptual fog, rendering opinions and beliefs obviously identifiable, expanding my understanding, and opening an awareness of my response-ability in any given circumstance. In order to bring my attention to the present moment, first, I aim to name the materially obvious in as few words as possible.

Ask yourself:

Question: Where is my current experience taking place right now? Where is my body?

Be as specific as possible in naming your physical location. Notice that you vibrate differently and respond differently to different locations. Also, depending on your emotional investment in your current circumstance, your opinion about where you are is tinted. Aim to leave out all coloring and instead, like a technician, sterilely identify your current location.

Example:

I am in the dirtiest room of the house. (Tinted by opinion.)

I am in the kitchen. (Clear and concise.)

Question: Who else is here with me? With whom/what am I communicating or interacting?

Be as specific as possible in naming the entities with whom you interact, be they animate or inanimate. Name them either by their known name or by your relationship to them. Notice how different titles, words, and names bring forth various responses within your nervous system. Notice also that your willingness to identify others clearly and nonemotionally may be influenced by your perception of the experience. Be precise with your words. Aim to capture the other entity/entities honestly in a few concise words that mean something to you.

Example:

I am word-battling with filthy miniature mess-makers. (Tinted by opinion.)

I am communicating with my children. (Clear and concise.)

Question: About what, precisely? What am I expressing, discussing, sharing, exchanging? What is the subject at hand?

Be as non-opinionated as possible as you identify the exchange at hand. Notice how the mind likes to name things according to its mood, perspective, wants, and desires. Aim to disengage from your opinions and instead stick to the bare facts at hand. Instead of casting a critical eye over the event at hand, open your vision of it and enjoy including only the essentials.

Example:

They're deflecting my orders to bathe with gross bathroom humor. (Tinted by opinion.)

We're discussing bodily functions and bathing. (Clear and concise, just the facts.)

Marrying all of the facts together, ask yourself:

Question: *What is actually happening in this present moment? What are the circumstances within which I find myself?*

Answer: *I am in the dirtiest room of the house, word-battling with filthy miniature mess-makers who deflect my orders to bathe with gross bathroom humor. (Tinted by opinion.)*

I am in the kitchen with my children, discussing bodily functions and bathing. (Clear and concise.)

Leave off all embellishments and interpretations, even when what is being said/done is apparently contradictory. Aim to identify the moment as factually, precisely, and inclusively as possible in one phrase, using as few words as possible.

As plain as it may at first feel, precisely identifying what is truthfully happening will facilitate higher, clearer, more veracious intentions. With an accurate and genuine comprehension of what is going on, you are more likely to remain loyal to your intent. This phrase doesn't have to be particularly exciting, fascinating, or stimulating; it simply has to be truthful and accurate.

Practice this for fun:

Remove your mind's identification with the experience by removing the first-person pronoun from your definition of what is happening. Replace the "*I am*" in your phrase with the third person form of "*She is*" or "*He is*" or even more liberating: "*It is*" or "*They are.*" Notice the leap of amusement your heart transmits as perceptions expand. This suggestion is not about gender roles or sexual preferences; it is about self-liberation from titles and perceptions. When you are in a circumstance charged with emotion, it can be incredibly freeing to cognize in the third person. Feel the vibrational variations of the following statements:

Example: *I am in the kitchen with my children, discussing bodily functions and bathing.*

Ex.: *He is in the kitchen with his children, discussing bodily functions and bathing.*

Go even further:

Remove all references to ownership or possession from the phrase. Objects and entities are no longer "*mine*," "*ours*" or "*yours*" and instead remain in the Infinite State of "*a*" or "*the*" articulation.

> *Example:* He is in the kitchen with the children, discussing bodily functions and bathing.

Once you arrive at a clear and accurate comprehension of what is currently Truthfully occurring, you can build upon that awareness.

Deepen your quest for understanding by further developing your formula:

> **Question:** *What is my (her/his/its/their) active intention in this exchange/event/happening?*
>
> **Objectively ask:** *What is the essential, primary intent of "being in the kitchen with children discussing bodily functions and bathing"?*
>
> This is the actual active intention to embody.
>
> **Example:**
>
> He intends to bathe the children.
>
> He wants the children to bathe.
>
> His objective is to get the children bathed.

By naming the indispensable ideal outcome in the third person, we rid ourselves of any emotional or intellectual misperceptions we may be tempted to contribute to the exchange. The circumstances may very well include an emotional reality, which we prefer to leave out of our understanding of what is occurring. Emotions are what we can consider a "given" and are not reliable as a lone resource. It is much wiser and way more creative to respond to Life from an able, open, and empowered position than from an unstable, biased stance.

For example, he most likely cares for the children he intends on getting bathed. However, if he concentrates his efforts on communicating the emotion of paternal devotion, his communication will be cloudy at best. If instead he focuses his attention on his intention, his Intuition will expand and his exchange, his communication, will be not only more *creative/inventive*, it will also be clearer and more efficient. Emotions are not within our control, whereas getting the little people under our care to bathe, quite possibly, is.

The exchange will have an Energetic Reality of its own accord, spontaneously birthed in the moment between the individuals engaged in it. According to how one Intuits the progress or success of their intention, an emotional reaction may occur. We sustain the *wisdom* of our Intuition by allowing an authentic response to arise in response to what we observe. Our perspective then becomes of the utmost importance, for it is from there that we will either observe *Infinite* possibilities or unending limits.

If he willingly and fully commits himself to the active intention of getting the children bathed, his *love* for them, if present, will be self-evident. There is no right or wrong intention for any circumstance or experience. We are free to decide for ourselves how we choose to be what we are.

Our exploration is around mindful presence, an awareness of what is going on in and around us in the ever-blossoming present.

> *"Whatever the present moment contains, accept it as if you had chosen it. Always work with it, not against it."*
>
> — ECKHART TOLLE

FOR LOVE OF THE NOW

It is said that all suffering originates in one's perception of circumstances, in one's associations with the "context" of *Life*. Therefore, my aim is to lessen my attachment to the intellect, for a heightened sensitivity only available in the Now. Once I'm able to objectively identify the context I am experiencing, I become able to expand my awareness beyond it. I am free to continue exploring and embodying what is Eternally True about me, conditions and environment aside.

Present-moment awareness reinforces my ability to respond as Truthfully as possible regardless of the circumstances within which I happen to find myself. Mystics say that beyond our interpretation of this Life experience, there is *an Energetic Source of Immeasurable Benevolence, Infinitude, Abundance, Purity, Light, Joy,* and *Love*. If I observe Life from this perspective, purposely recognizing It as an *Eternal*,

Infinitely Creative Reality, and I invest in the unknowable *Wisdom* of that All-Encompassing Love Force, as Life... what arises is a *joyful, brilliant* opportunity to be as One with All That Is.

We are wholly created and made to create. We are, by Nature, Creatively Enabled. This is a solid foundation from which to express our Authentic Self Truthfully in the always-unfolding Now. When I embrace my *Unique Embodiment of Immeasurable Potential*, a childlike sensation of playfulness ignites. I know the Truth by how It resonates. A "sacred yes" always feels like precisely what it is.

Just as with any new practice, your focus may wander, and your ability to concentrate might need some development and support. In those moments when I notice my attention roaming, I gently guide my awareness to the Now, to my feet on the ground, my rear end in the chair, and my breath moving through my vessel, nourishing my heart-center.

The physical reality within which we interact is made of form that exists in three dimensions: height, width, and depth. Thoughts originate in a dimension that is beyond weight and height and depth, and yet, we've all experienced thoughts that seem heavy, massive, and profound. Seductive and mesmerizing, repetitive thoughts collect to form energetic thought entities. As weightless as they may appear at first glance, even our thoughts demand our attention, they insist we follow them and often we do. Sometimes, we follow thoughts so far as to get lost, losing the plot in thought, and find ourselves (mentally, emotionally, and Spiritually) somewhere other than here in the ever-flourishing Now.

> *"Now is the only reality. All else is either memory or imagination."*
>
> — OSHO

With intention, I learned how to redirect my focus, bringing my awareness to the Now without judging or punishing myself for having lost my way. The time I waste criticizing myself for my wandering attention is just more time I spend away from the Presence all around me; that *is* me. If I continually practice returning my attention to where it belongs, where it best serves me and the world, eventually, it reveals itself as a preferred State of Being.

You need not become more perceptive to nurture your Presence in the present Now into a talent; instead, practice observing and responding to your Intuitions, revealed only in the moment, as to fully embrace and embody what Life is offering you at any given point. There is never any need to make anything up in the present. Now, there's nothing to invent. We choose instead to reveal the Truth as we understand it.

> *"You are the Now, in essence. On the surface, the Now is what happens; in the depths of Now, the Now is the space in which it happens. So that which happens is the*

world of form, coming and going and coming and going... and the space in which it happens is the unconditioned, formless, timeless, the unborn, the uncreated, the un-manifested, pure consciousness itself: the one, or the light of the one. And so, be the Now, be the space for what happens, rather than continuously reacting to what happens and being hypnotized by the world of form."

— Eckhart Tolle

Active awareness

Availability towards our deepest Internal and Universal Truths gifts us with massive insight. Spiritual self-awareness is an unending well of information and the way to nurture a healthy sense of connectedness to All of Life, ourselves included. Our willingness to tap into what connects us all is a courageous, *wisdom*-manifesting act of *free* choice. We cannot help but become more *united* with All of Life as we connect with our Inner Self, thus nurturing a sagacity that goes beyond intellectualization. The challenges I faced when practicing awareness, beyond my availability, had to do with fearful projections based on my belief systems.

When I first began to nourish my ability to stay present non-judgmentally, it was easy to maintain awareness during moments of relaxation or when engaged in enjoyable activities, like walking in Nature or listening to calming music. However, when faced with what I perceived as a stressful situation or a conflict in my personal relationships, I would struggle to sustain a *balanced* level of awareness. In those moments of heightened emotion or discomfort, my fear levels would increase, setting off a shift in my vibrational field or energetic state of being. As a result, it became quite challenging to prioritize my True Self and my sense of Presence; at times, I'd even go so far as to resist being aware. My intellect would take over, as it tends to try to do when a threat is perceived, encouraging me to stay safe in reactivity based on thoughtless, habitual patterns or automatic responses ingrained in my belief system.

The value and importance I was able to assign to my awareness seemed to vary according to my vibrational field or my energetic state of being. I noticed a tendency of preferring to practice awareness in moments of low stress or in circumstances where I didn't feel challenged, upset, or uncomfortable. This is very natural at first and is nothing to be ashamed of or to hold ourselves prisoner over. Noticing my habitual neurological patterns lovingly and with compassion facilitated the necessary, organic upgrade in my awareness. What starts as a practice soon matures into a state of Consciousness, especially when *loving*-kindness is a constant companion of the practitioner.

When you feel frightened, anxious, depressed, or uneasy, observe yourself to see if you tend to lean on impulsiveness and not Intuition. Compassionately consider if you've ever mistaken survival-based instincts for your True Nature. In those instances, you may notice yourself more in a state of reaction than in one of response.

"Awareness is like the sun. When it shines on things, they are transformed."

— THICH NHAT HANH

I can mislead myself if I behave, think, and form beliefs from a position of reactivity. How I interpret information reveals the difference between an impulse and an intuition. The choices I make based on what I perceive reveal to me whether I am behaving intuitively or instinctively. I can feel it in my body. Because it is *Unconditional*, Intuition feels similar to Love. It is a responsive way of being, not a reactive way. It is Internal and speaks to me from within; it is my *Innate Wisdom*, and Its voice is deeper, softer, and larger than the voice of my personality, whose tones vibrate in the head.

"The only tyrant I accept in this world is the 'still small voice' within me. And even though I have to face the prospect of being a minority of one, I humbly believe I have the courage to be in such a hopeless minority."

— MAHATMA MOHANDAS K. GANDHI

While instincts lack consideration for us and others, Intuition is selfless and doesn't serve personal gain. We can access our gorgeous and wise Intuition through listening and sensing, in stillness or in movement, in silence or not. Impulses are of the physical realm and ask us to take action, to *do* something, in order to bring them to fruition.

Curious for a greater understanding of the human condition, I, like so many before me, ask myself with *loving* availability: why do I do what I do?

Thanks to profound explorations into my own existentialism, I observe certain pervading human recurrences, one of which is that we tend to be fundamentally afraid of being unloved. As a child and young adult, I carried a deep belief that I was not loved or lovable; perhaps you can relate. The evidence of this fear being a worldwide human perception is fairly obvious. In honoring my self-explorations, I trust the revelations unearthed in my ongoing and profound observation of the species. Upon slightly deeper inquiry, it becomes clear that some of us will go to extremes, doing just about anything to be and to feel loved, to hear someone say to us: I love you, you are loved, you are lovable.

I love you. You are loved. You are lovable. ~Jen

A personal example of Love-seeking that brought me to the realization that I had learned to abandon myself and my needs arose during an important theater production in which I was the lead actor. During that period, I was heavily involved in various activities, from working full-time to studying various healing modalities to co-running a theater company while collaborating with a troupe of thespians, often taking on leadership roles and saying yes to every request for help or involvement. While I appeared successful and accomplished on the surface, internally, I was overwhelmed and constantly exhausted. Despite feeling drained and stretched thin, I continued to accept every opportunity that came my way out of fear of disappointing others or being perceived (by my own inner critic) as incapable.

In particular, we were in what's called "tech rehearsals" the week of the play's opening. I had committed to organizing our opening night event and to hand-writing every single "thank you" note that was to be sent to every single patron despite already feeling swamped with professional and personal responsibilities. As opening night approached, an event happened within the troupe that added to what felt like mounting chaos. Our company director had come in early to find several actors had carelessly left their costumes on the dressing room floor. Far from professional behavior, it incited a furious verbal explosion directed at each and every company member. Rest assured, Dear Life Artist; my costumes were neatly and respectfully hung in my dressing room; however, this fact was entirely irrelevant to the one offended. The verbal volcano erupted all over each one of us, the whole of us, delivering sharp accusations and violent pronunciations. I silently yielded to his anger and felt no need to defend myself. Instead, I tapped into my compassionate heart and contemplated what I would say and how I would say it were I in his shoes. It was his delivery that I had issue with, not his professional stance on how handsewn costumes must be treated.

The next morning, I awoke with no voice. It was the day before opening night, and our lead was voiceless. Thankfully, my support job happened to be working in a holistic wellness center amongst some of the most powerful healers I've ever had the privilege of knowing. Several practitioners came to my rescue, providing immediate resources, applications, and self-care solutions. One colleague in particular, while having me roll my socked feet on tennis balls, a soothing Reflexology practice, gently whispered in my ear, "Jennifer... What are you not saying? Have you kept yourself silent lately when you needed to speak up?" I nodded. She continued, "Whatever it is you are not expressing, sweetheart, you *must* say it." And immediately, I knew although my ego would have loved to cast blame on the harsh ways I'd been spoken to, unfairly and so fiercely, and to defend my goodness, my Inner Knower showed me myself as the one responsible for my missing voice.

The production ended up being a grand success, and I was able to deliver at my standard of performance every single night of the run. My voice returned on time, kindly nurtured by self-Loving practices, an extensive vocal warm-up, and the epiphany that arose instantly when I was asked about what I was keeping silent. In that instant, I realized that I had prioritized what I perceived as the needs and expectations of others over my own, ultimately abandoning myself in the process. This understanding was a wake-up call, prompting me to reevaluate my own priorities and learn to set healthy boundaries that honor my own self-care and well-being.

We're all on this beautiful journey to experience Love and we all want to be happy. It's a ubiquitous longing that connects us all. When we embrace ourselves and each other with compassion, we tap into the very essence of Love. Just imagine: Love isn't something external; it's already within us, an essential part of who we are at our core. And when we fully grasp this and understand that Love is Inherent in and as us, it opens the door to Reality, delivering True happiness.

> *"As above, so below, as within, so without, as the universe, so the soul..."*
>
> — Hermes Trismegistus

Now. Let's ponder something precious together: authenticity. What does it mean to be authentic? In a world packed with behavioral and belief conditioning, from our upbringing, our experiences, cultural and societal expectations, finding our authentic selves can feel like a wild adventure in itself. But amidst all this, there is a gorgeous Truth waiting to be uncovered: our Authentic Self is already within us, waiting to be acknowledged, embraced and celebrated. So, who are we, really? Let's continue to explore together.

As a social Spiritual Being, my general aim was to get along, fit in, like and be liked, make friends, and be accepted or approved of, first at home, then at school, then in the workplace, attempting to be happy, to keep peace, to please, to impress, to achieve, to succeed and thrive. In doing so, I put myself at risk of going through a period of my Life wearing a mask and playing characters that were caricatures of my Authentic Self. Playing a role kept me from my Inner Nature, throwing me out of *balance*, as I so fully experienced when my voice escaped me. In that mindset, I was simply in service of a superficial belief system that encouraged me to construct characters and play roles that led me away from my inherent state of happiness.

On the upward spiral of self-awareness there is profound *peace* found in the striping away of those beliefs and those masks; it is a lifting of the veils that reveals our True Inner Essence. It can be unbearably painful work because in releasing those roles, we sometimes realize that we are more familiar with our Character than with our own inner voice.

> *"The privilege of a lifetime is to become who you truly are."*
>
> — CARL JUNG

What follows are a few contemplations to ponder around possible conditioned beliefs, behaviors, or ideas you may have picked up along the way. I suggest you consider these queries without attaching any need to know and with honor for whatever arises as insight.

Allow yourself to Intuit a bit without grasping for answers.

- What were the first impressions, the first interpretations of Life I experienced?
- What are the interpretations, the perceptions of Life I return to again and again, for pleasure or for pain?
- What roles did I invent to gain approval or to be treated with kindness?
- What mask did I wear for my safety or protection?
- What characters did I take on to gain respect or to feel Love?
- What repetitive emotions and behaviors do I evoke and put to use, by habit or as a conditioned response to Life?
- What if I...Take off the mask, release the role, strip the character down until all that's left is my True Essence?
- Who would I be now, and what would be True about me were I to liberate myself from learned, limiting beliefs about my capacity, my abilities, my Natural gifts, Innate blessings, and Inherent talents?

Let's willingly go deeper, beyond our upbringing, beyond our autobiography, beyond beliefs, beyond conditioning, beyond identity, even beyond thoughts and feelings, into our core of pure Conscious Awareness. Our Core, where self-worth, self-image, self-Love, and All Knowingness reside. From here, from the roots to the core, from this spaciousness and infinitude, we cleanse ourselves of contradictions within our opinions, releasing them for Truth, True Nature, and Authentic Self.

Self-Balance Guided Meditation

In the following guided meditation practice, you'll explore the Spiritual aptitude known as "equanimity", which is the willingness to remain present, steady, and grounded when Life becomes challenging or when your Protective Personality has taken the wheel and is driving your sense of awareness out of balance. This practice cultivates a Consciousness of, and a relationship with, our Internal Harmony, Peace, and Order. I've chosen to share it now to encourage a sense of safety while you continue to deepen your self-knowing.

Sit comfortably in a quiet place where you won't be disturbed. Your spine is erect and aligned but not strained in any way; you are alert and relaxed.

Close your eyes and bring your attention to the movement of breath in and through your body temple. Breathe quietly and patiently, in and out, through your nose.

Recall that equanimity arises through continued mindfulness. Be mindful right here and right now of sensation in your body temple. Be mindful, here and now, of movement or changes in your breathing. Be mindful, always, of activity in your mind itself.

And now, make a commitment to remain aware of body, breath, and mind in each moment as you contemplate the following pairs of words:

The first pair is Praise and Blame. Contemplate the reaction in your body temple or in your mind when someone compliments you. In what ways do compliments throw you off balance? And what would it feel like to receive a compliment and yet, remain stable in body, breath, and mind? And when you receive criticism? In what ways do you lose your balanced state of mind? And is it possible to receive criticism and, with mindful awareness, remain present and undisturbed? How does your body temple respond to praise? And how does it respond to blame? Be present with the sensations that arise as you sit with the concepts of praise and blame.

(Pause for 3-5 breaths)

Now, consider the duo of Gain and Loss. What arises in your body temple, and mind when you reflect upon gain and loss? Do you feel pushed or pulled in any one direction? Reflect briefly upon an experience when you got exactly what you wanted. Now recall an experience when you lost something dear to you. What would it feel like to hold space equally for joy and the suffering? Notice in the body temple what it might be like to extend warmth and love equally to your "wins" and your "losses" and to all of the sensations those two things evoke.

(Pause for 3-5 breaths)

Now, bring to your awareness the duo of Pleasure and Pain. What arises? Are you aware of an attachment to pleasure and an aversion to pain? Or, in some ways, do you avoid pleasure and grasp onto your pain? What would it feel like in your body temple to equally welcome all sensations? To allow for the fullness of your human experience without attachment to any of it? What surfaces for you as you contemplate pleasure and pain?

(Pause for 3-5 breaths)

Now, reflect upon Fame and Ill Repute. In what ways are you thrown off balance by what others think of you? Notice the push and the pull of popularity, recognition, acknowledgment, and notoriety. Notice, too, how the body temple reacts to disrespect, dishonor, disregard, or neglect. Notice where attachment lies, where your mind or your body gets stuck. Notice where your body temple is holding, where it feels tight, and where and why it begins to soften, to open up.

(Pause for 3-5 breaths)

Now, turn your attention back to your seat, back to the connection between your hips, your legs, or your feet and the Earth. Turn your attention towards the steadiness and ease of your breath. With each exhalation, feel yourself even more grounded, rooted, and stable.

Like an ancient tree in the forest, you are firmly rooted. Your strong foundation has grown deeper, more powerful, over time. Sure, the weather may change, the wind may pick up, and you can be pushed and pulled to and fro... but no condition is strong enough to uproot you.

You bend, you sway, but you keep returning to center, never angry at the clouds for passing through and never pining for a sunny day. You accept it all as it is, understanding that you could sometimes use the rain.

All is welcome. You remain stable, rooted in your awareness. Awareness is the home base from which you grow. You are stable, balanced, harmonious, strong, and free.

Sit with whatever arises in practice for as long as you like, and return to this meditation as often as would serve you to do so or whenever a sense of equanimity would be of value to you.

I realize that I receive information from three Interior sources: Instinctively through my senses, Intellectually through my mind, and Intuitively through my Core. In exploring the interconnectedness of my Innate Intelligence, I have come to understand that in order for me to access my deeply rooted *wisdom*, not only must these three Interior resources communicate, they must be united and working in collaboration.

INTERNAL INFORMATION SOURCES

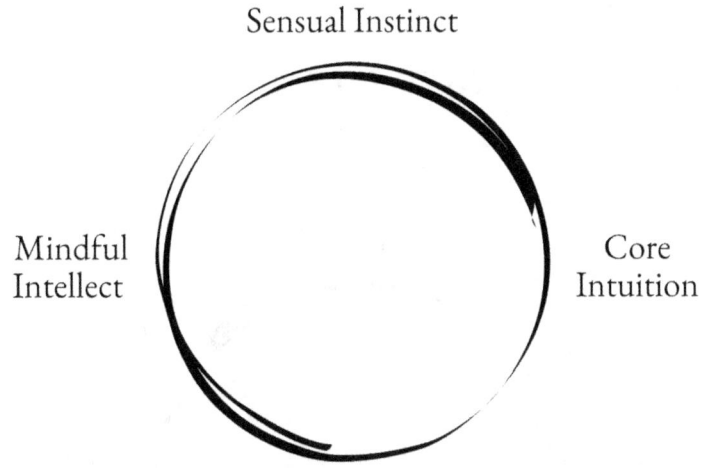

I definitely notice that when my interior sources are at their best, utter *brilliance* and *originality* are more than probable. On these *glorious* occasions, there truly is space for *infinite* possibility and continual realization: I might even define these experiences as opportunities for the miraculous to take place. The Masterpiece of each individual Life is created within. This is the marriage of mind, body, and Spirit we've all heard speak of.

> "Love art in yourself and not yourself in art."
>
> — CONSTANTIN STANISLAVSKI

Intuition Ignition

Inspiration manifests in Intuition, which informs intention, which collaborates with action.

INTUITION'S PATH TO ACTION

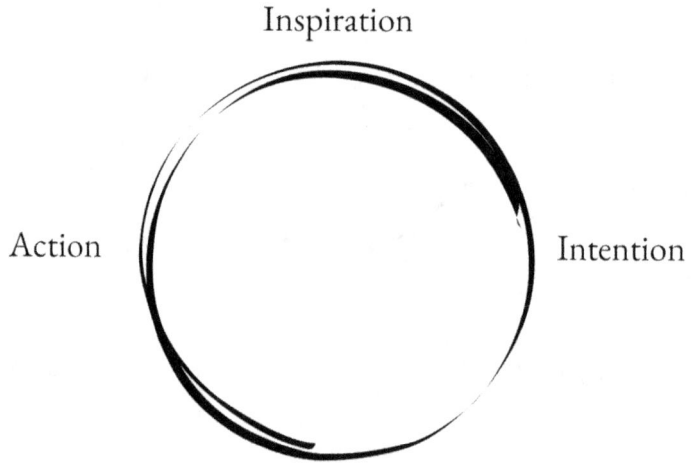

The creative impulse takes the form of inspiration for me; an instinct transforms into an idea, sparking the ignition of my intuition. I feel incited, and as I observe, I become aware that I am actually receiving energetic signals from within. I can elevate those vibrations to a higher frequency, enabling me to decipher the information they provide. At this point, typically, my mind translates my impulses into words, forming thoughts. I embrace my material mind as an asset when collaborating with my Inner Wisdom. Within my

Being, a concert is taking place between my body temple, in the form of physical senses, my mind, in the form of thoughts, and my Energy Body is formless but highly communicative nonetheless. I embody awareness as to help sustain the *beautiful* sense of *harmony* shared by these energetic realities. Thus, when an Intuition wants to manifest itself into intention, I am able to live and interact while remaining true to my *loving* nature.

"There is a voice that doesn't use words. Listen"

— RUMI

Living and working authentically requires me to connect to my core; I must tap into my Inner Wisdom in order to courageously live with intention. If my beliefs and thoughts create my interpretations of my experiences, my Inner Wisdom suggests: "I am Infinitely Creative and Intuitive" as a possible point of view. My mind and ego may resist this option, reminding me that *infinitude* seems to be something outside of myself. And I honor that suggestion; infinitude is not within the linear version of reality, the time-space continuum I play and have my Being in. Infinitude resides within me, profoundly etched in our shared Consciousness. I happen to embody it because, like you, I am it. I am *Infinitude* temporarily incarnate, if you will, and I propose you are as well.

Once, when I was about ten years old, during a wander through the woods, I stumbled upon a small clearing bathed in sunlight. As I stood there, surrounded by towering trees and the gentle rustle of leaves, I couldn't help but feel a sense of awe and wonder at the Beauty of Nature. At that moment, it struck me how infinitude is not just a concept but a tangible presence in our world.

As I gazed up at the sky, I marveled at the vastness of the Universe and the countless stars that twinkle above me at night. Those stars are always there, whether I see them or not. I realized that I was but a tiny speck in the grand scheme of things while also possessing unknown potential within me. Reflecting on this, I understood that we are *Infinitely Creative Beings*; the possibilities that lie before us are truly *immeasurable*, and the ways in which we can express ourselves are countless. Just as Nature manifests in myriad forms, so too can we tap into our Inner Life Artistry and bring forth something *unique* and *beautiful* into the world.

In that moment of clarity, I felt a deep sense of gratitude for the gift of Existence and the boundless potential that resides within each and every one of us. It was a humbling reminder that I am not separate from the Universe but intrinsically connected to it and that the expression of *Infinitude* is not confined to the Cosmos but can be found right here in the Earth realm. My entire incarnation as Jennifer has been a remembrance of that illuminating Truth: my Oneness with All That Is.

Inner Wisdom suggests that we are *Infinitely Creative* and Innately, organically Intuitive. Whatever enlivens our heart is our gateway to the natural gifts bestowed upon us through Intelligence. Intuitively, we communicate with our core Wisdom guided by the Light of the Soulful heart-center, without which we wouldn't be able to perceive our Essence.

Listening with the *whole* Self is more than what our ears can hear or eyes can see; it is a Sacred State of Being that involves responses from our senses, our observations, and our Intuition. Listening fully means sensing what we see, hear, taste, feel, and smell, all that we perceive internally and externally, from within our *whole* and *complete* core, and allowing it, honoring it truthfully, no matter the circumstances within which we happen to find ourselves. It's difficult at first to give ourselves completely over to sacred listening; we're often too distracted thinking of what our next line is or of our shopping list, or perhaps most painful of all, we are judging what is being revealed.

Truthfully, if we have the courage to listen fully, we already have access to all of the Intelligence and comprehension we will ever need. Those who put trust in listening receive things they would not have otherwise noticed. I'll share a story with you from my work as a Spiritual Counselor that may serve as an example of what I mean by "listening fully," which will be followed by an opportunity for you to practice sacred listening yourself.

While a client of mine shared his newfound sense of *freedom* after ending his long-term marriage, I couldn't help but notice the conflicting messages bubbling beneath the surface of his words. Despite his attempts to appear joyful and liberated, something unspoken was lingering in his tone and demeanor.

He had just ended a relationship that he had wanted to leave for a decade; he'd been married for over twenty years in what he often defined as a loveless, torturous marriage. He had invested a lot of fear and a lot of rage in that relationship, volatile emotions that demanded from him deliberate self-compassion, practiced in Spiritual counsel with me, to nurture the courage he needed to choose his own well-being over a promise he'd made that he no longer felt in alignment with. His perceptions about the relationship had kept him in a holding pattern, taking a great toll on his health, both physically and mentally. Besides needing serious care of his body, he also needed loving compassion for his mind, in honor and in service of his mighty Soul.

As he outwardly expressed to me his satisfaction at being free from what he described as a heartless and convoluted relationship, there was an underlying bitterness that belied his *true* feelings. As he spoke of his ex-wife cheerfully yet in disparaging terms, I sensed a mixture of resentment and pain lurking within him.

Despite his attempts to mask his inner turmoil with bravado, I chose to listen deeply, tuning in to the subtle nuances of his speech and his silences, witnessing his body language and feeling into his electromagnetic field. It became apparent that beneath his façade of liberation, he was grappling with a complex array of emotions: grief, anger, and even a deep sense of judgment around the guilt he felt for the years he'd invested in an unhappy marriage.

Rather than confronting or dismissing his contradictory words, I approached the situation with compassion and understanding. I recognized that his seemingly hostile remarks were not a *true* reflection of his innermost feelings but rather an emotional manifestation of the turmoil he had embodied for so long. By creating a safe space within which he could express himself without judgment and inviting him into some reflection practices, I was able to encourage him to delve deeper into his condensed energy (emotions) to uncover the underlying truths that lay beneath the surface. In doing so, he was able to express the complexity of his experience, lovingly facing himself full-on, as an act of self-honor and discovery, not limited by his mind's attempt to protect him through intellectualization and rationalized harsh judgment.

At once, he was able to tap into the healing consciousness known as forgiveness, a *loving* movement that was Internal and directed at himself. His tears flowed with wild abandon as he released what felt to him like tons of residual emotion. Gone were the biting terms of "right" or "wrong" and "good" or "bad", and in their place arose a vast opening from within, a tender, vulnerable, powerful *freedom* he had all but forgotten during a decade of blame and self-victimization.

Ultimately, our session that day served as a poignant reminder to me of the sacred value of profound listening and compassionate understanding in support of others on their journey toward healing and self-realization. Regardless of the harshness of his words, and notwithstanding the cheerfulness of his delivery, I remained steadfast in my commitment to guiding him toward greater self-awareness and Spiritual wellness. No matter what he shared, I sustained within my awareness the Truth of his (and his ex-wife's) essential *perfection, wholeness, goodness,* and *beauty*. The key ingredient: my willingness to listen beyond the surface.

Listening fully is not, by the way, something we embody only for, and when with, those we care about; it is an active state of being, like forgiveness, that we get to first master internally, within ourselves.

Full Listening

Stop what you are doing and pause.

Take a few deep rounds of breath, bringing more oxygen into your body.

Direct your attention to your Soulful heart-center,

not to where your physical heart resides, but to the right of it, in the center of your chest area.

Imagine breathing into and out of your heart-center.

Listen for all of the subtle information you will perceive as you inhale and exhale slowly, deeply, with calm alertness.

Listening generates reactions, but you are not reactive.

Observe. You are the Observer and the Observed: One Whole Integral Being.

Sacred listening is often neglected by those who tend to focus on the words.

When your intellect tries to distract or assist you, invite it to play with you, direct it to focus on your intention of listening.

Be the Listener and the Listened To.

Let all judgments fall to the side for something more Loving. Drop the roles of Judge and Jury, for they never suited you anyway.

Be responsive to the stimuli within. Listen with more than your inner ear, observe with more than your inner eye: give your Whole Being over to the act of sacred self-listening.

The "give and take" of Intelligence, Compassion, Wisdom, and Love Innately embodied within your Inner Life Artist is rich, full, real, and powerful beyond imagination.

Listen. Receive. Be present with your Whole Being.

If an honest response emerges, acknowledge it, accept it unconditionally, and allow it to be.

Keep breathing into and out of your beautiful and mighty heart-center.

Gently be aware of what you are experiencing, sensing, feeling, noticing, and revealing.

Try not to guide, or adjust, or alter any aspect of yourself. Instead, be with your Dear Companion, your Intuition, for it will support and inform your greatest intentions.

Ask yourself: What is the most important aspect of my Life right now?

"The intuitive mind is a sacred gift, and the rational mind is a faithful servant. We have created a society that honors the servant and has forgotten the gift."

— Albert Einstein

Authenticity in Action

In the contemplation of releasing attachments, beliefs, and outdated aspects of one's identity, the ego may perceive a threat, prompting it to retreat and attempt to conceal the Inner Genius. The narratives and language utilized in self-expression have the potential to temporarily confine, prior to emancipating, the Life Artist within. Spiritual/Human Beings are magnificent, magical, and miraculous creations, and disregarding this Truth diminishes self-worth, leading to a loss of self-respect, encouraging a sense of disconnection from our profound Inner Brilliance.

Our beliefs sculpt our version of reality, influencing our perceptions of our past, present, and future. Gaining familiarity with our beliefs through sacred listening of our stories, words, and vocabulary opens a gateway, a threshold into *boundless* potential in an *expansive*, unforeseen future. We are invited, as it is our *Innate Creative* right and our *Supreme* capability, to recognize the interplay between self, narratives, language, and thoughts, which in turn influence beliefs, behaviors, and ultimately, reality. This creative prowess stands as the cornerstone of a profoundly *joyous* existence.

Continuing on this path, when we confine ourselves to purely intellectual perceptions, we limit ourselves to the boundaries of our minds, restricting our potential and playing small. The logical, goal-oriented nature of the mind imposes limitations, offering only a narrow view of what is possible based solely on past experiences and references. As we embark on new ventures, we may find ourselves plagued by worries about our abilities and capabilities, reflecting the mind's finite perspective. Just as likely, we may find ourselves defensively boastful, arrogant and superficially overconfident, reflecting the ego's protective instinct in action.

Yet, our capacity is not the true obstacle; rather, it is our own sense of self-worth that holds us back. Deep-seated doubts about whether we deserve the fulfillment of our heart's desires, our Intuition's Guidance, and our Soul's calling often torment us. These doubts, usually unspoken and subconscious, question our worthiness of the *magnificence* seeking expression through us, as us, and whether we have the right to claim it.

While the inclination to nurture our Authentic Self is strong, we may find ourselves grappling with deeply ingrained blocks that hinder our progress. It is essential to cultivate the ability to identify these doubts, assumptions, reactions, and emotions of inadequacy within ourselves. By acknowledging and sitting with them, we can begin to release them in favor of a Higher Truth. Confronting the reality of the present moment, regardless of how challenging it may seem, is crucial. Embracing what is, and allowing it to be, is the pathway to accessing our *Innate Intelligence* and welcoming Its guidance and insights.

Letting go of what no longer serves us, releasing the falsehoods we've been conditioned to believe, is a powerful act of intentional self-liberation. It frees not only ourselves but also our imagination and our *innate* creativity. By shedding the identities and beliefs imposed upon us by worldly society, we open the door to something greater, something more authentic.

I invite you to welcome the True Essence of yourself into the forefront of your awareness and allow it to guide you on your life's journey.

> *"Authenticity is the daily practice of letting go of who we think we are supposed to be and embracing who we actually are."*
>
> — BRENÉ BROWN

Exercising Authenticity

Find a quiet space where you will not be disturbed for twenty minutes.

Get settled where you can sit comfortably. Keep your journal and something to write with close by.

If possible, sit with your feet firmly grounded on the floor, your spine aligned, and your sit bones supporting you where they come in contact with your chair or meditation cushion.

Check-in with your body and notice any tension you may be holding onto.

Take a few deep breaths, giving your entire body weight over to the Earth below.

Creating space through your breath, expand your stomach as you inhale, and contract it as you exhale.

Follow this internal movement for three full rounds of breath.

Feel the Earth beneath you, supporting you. Releasing into It anything that no longer serves you as you allow your breath to flow naturally.

Smell the air surrounding you and notice if you can taste anything.

Listen to your environment.

With each inhalation, invite forgiveness, appreciation, celebration, and wellness. Create space within.

With each exhalation let go of shame, regret, resentments, judgements, criticisms. Let it go.

Continue with this practice for three full rounds of breath. Creating space as the body temple inhales and surrendering what doesn't serve as the body temple exhales.

Notice your body temperature, and once again, scan your physical body temple for tension.

Breathe deeply and with the intention to release and relax.

Notice your thoughts, notice your mood.

Observe any words, stories, or beliefs as they float by and through your awareness.

Release any need to know.

Accept that all is well. There is nothing you have to do or be. There is nowhere to go. Remain present with yourself.

Bring your attention to your breathing: without controlling your breath, simply acknowledge its presence with a nod of gratitude.

Direct your attention to your heart-center... place a hand there in self-recognition.

Compassionately listen as your Authentic Self finishes the following sentences:

- No matter what people think, I know...
- Integrity in my life looks like...

- What gives me the highest energetic charge is...
- I am pulled towards...
- I am most myself when I...

"Every good painter paints what he is." ~

— JACKSON POLLOCK

Living in Intention

"We all have the power... we've just forgotten how to use it. Intentions give us the pathway to consciously create our lives."

— Kim Stanwood Terranova

In the fascinating realm of intentions, there is an eye-opening *Truth*: we are incessantly setting intentions, often without realizing it. We are constantly exchanging energy, emitting photons (light) in an ongoing conversation with everything. An energetic web, or communication system, connects us all. We transmit and receive simultaneously and in every moment. All day, every day, we are in an invisible discourse with everything around us, as well as with ourselves. Inevitably, a silent inner monologue, our ongoing stream of endless thoughts, becomes our Life's quality, that which we perceive and experience. Thoughts, as it turns out, are subtle agents of intention, and every thought we have is a silent message to Creative Consciousness, influencing our perceptions of reality. This is how our intentions manifest into our experiences; we actually fulfill our thoughts, whether we are aware of it or not. Our thoughts are contagious. What we send out comes back to us magnified. A great contemplation is to ponder what we are broadcasting at any particular moment in our day.

> *"When the time comes that nothing goes forth from you other than that which you would be glad to have returned, then you will have reached your heaven."*
>
> — ERNEST HOLMES

The brain doesn't discriminate between a thought and an action, a detail that can become a powerful ally when we live and act intentionally. It can allow us to engage in the Art of Mental Rehearsal, much like professional athletes, executives, musicians and actors do, exponentially enhancing the likelihood of our intentions materializing into form and experience. By focusing on our active intention, we direct our vitality, our Life energy, in that direction toward its fulfillment.

> *"Where the mind goes, energy flows."*
>
> — ERNEST HOLMES

To have intent is to Consciously *be*, with purpose, activating specifics around behaviors, movements, tone, delivery, vibrational exchanges, thoughts, visions, and creative potential. An intention is identified through an awareness of an ideal state of being. The current popular belief system calls this ideal outcome a "goal." For those who are prepared for an intention to manifest itself instantly, an ideal way of being can also be considered an Intention.

Intention, I have found, is different than the outdated practice of goal setting, for when we set goals, our vision narrows, our imagination shrinks, the field of possibilities diminishes, disempowering our Life Artist and stifling Its fullest *magnificence* from emerging into expression. Intention setting, instead, allows for greater possibilities, for something new and never before seen to occur, for changes and shifts to flow with *ease*, and for our vision to remain wide-open as to perceive a vast field of potential beyond our imagination. Intention liberates and empowers the Life Artist to a deeper realization of one's Innate *brilliance*.

Beyond our invisible but still very perceptible energetic field, it is through our actions, behaviors, and words that we consistently embody our intentions. Being selective about our actions, based on our intentions, rooted in an ideal state of being, is an invaluable ability we can all develop with a bit of conscious practice. Let's explore some of the characteristics of living in intention, of being actively intentional.

An active intention is in alignment with an ideal outcome, which has its own qualities.

We actually set intentions rooted in specific qualities inspired by (but not attached to) an ideal outcome. This subtle detail is essential and can be supported by our awareness of the circumstances from moment to moment. Once we arrive at a quality, our intention is realized through whatever we express as, in service of that reality. How we communicate, relate, perceive, and behave all serve the realization of our intention.

Recently, there was a scenario in my Life where my intention was to comfort a student, and the ideal physical outcome was a shared hug. My intention allowed me to position my consciousness quite specifically, allowing me to reach out and interact with my student warmly, with genuine care and concern. As soon as we began our exchange, I could sense a deep connection and understanding between us. It felt as if our Soulful Selves were communicating through my consciously intentional actions, words, and behaviors, which were being present-moment guided by a desired outcome of connectivity and Love. The physical manifestation of a hug was not my goal; it was merely a powerful guidance coordinate being sustained by my Inner Creative Genius, a north star on my compass, if you will.

In service of this ideal outcome, various ideas naturally arose within me in the moment. I offered words of reassurance and encouragement, creating a peaceful and inviting environment to facilitate authentic, open communication and emotional release. As I successfully comforted this individual, I noticed a flooding of compassion filling my Being; my state of being was *peaceful* and *loving*. There was a profound warmth and lightness in my heart as I embodied the expressions of comfort and support. My intention had aligned harmoniously with the desired outcome, empowering me with the ability to provide solace to someone I care deeply about.

On the other hand, there was a moment in my Life when my intention was to correct an acquaintance, but my ideal outcome was a *peaceful* resolution. I found myself engaged in what was shaping up to become an argument, fueled by the desire to prove my point and assert my perspective.

As the conflict escalated, I could sense the tension building within me. My tone became increasingly pointed, my word choice more confrontational, and my posture rigid with defensiveness. Despite my ideal outcome of establishing a resolution, I found myself invested in a desire to win the argument. In the midst of the confrontation, I realized that my actions were jeopardizing the *peaceful* outcome I had envisioned. My insistence on correcting the other person only fueled the flames of conflict, creating a barrier to understanding and mutual respect.

In the midst of this experience, I recognized the importance of aligning my intentions with my desired outcomes. I realized the value of fostering open communication and seeking common ground was my actual intention, not to prove either of us right or wrong. By staying present with what was occurring and adapting my intention in the moment, I quickly released my willingness to argue to instead embrace the possibility of *peaceful* resolution, allowing me to navigate and communicate with greater compassion.

Aligning our intention to its quality is the way to avoid this type of miscommunication with ourselves and so-called others and lessen the frequency with which we betray our internal Life Artist. It is of the utmost importance to honor our ever-communicative Inner Wisdom as the ongoing, interactive, and flexible Intelligence it is.

An active intention has a specific outcome in mind but is not focused on it.

An ideal outcome is the ultimate manifestation of our actions, symbolizing the completion of any particular intention when we have realized what we set out to bring into existence. We understand that we've established an energetic connection by honoring ourselves and the other(s) with whom we are communicating or interacting. We feel, observe, and sensually comprehend through our relationship with the other; we observe it in them in the form of reflections, inflections, movements, vibrations, tones, and responses. If our intention is, for example, towards "establishing a trustworthy bond," we will sense its completion in the other person, people, or animal; it is their behaviors that inform us.

One of many ideal outcomes for the intention of establishing a trustworthy bond would be to get a handshake from the other(s) involved in said interaction. If, instead, we were to observe a calm, trusting, joyful smile in them, we'd know our intention was effective even though we hadn't achieved the physical outcome we'd envisioned. Likewise, were we to be so focused on our ideal outcome of getting a handshake that any other response would be viewed as a failure in communication, we'd be removed from the actual interaction, and our attention would be on the future outcome and not the present exchange. When we focus solely on the outcome or solely on our intention, we miss the information being provided to us by the second most stimulating, illuminating, revealing, and obvious source we have in front of us, perceiving only half of the communication: ours.

On the other hand, if our intention has no outcome in mind or is of a vague quality, we tend not to recognize progress or when new possibilities have arisen. For example, if our ideal, highest outcome is something like to "get along really well," which is vague, we risk never giving ourselves the opportunity to admit when vibrations rise, and productive exchanges occur. When exploring the specificities of the theatrical use of Intention, Konstantin Stanislavsky spoke of vagueness as being "the enemy of all art." Be specific with your intentions; know what their realization feels like.

Within any particular interaction or conversation, we may not achieve our desired outcome; however, being specific about its qualities allows our communications to flourish from a place of personal clarity.

An active intention does not aim to manipulate or control.

When our intention is to manufacture a reaction in ourselves or another person, when we aim to control the outcome of events, we are trying to create a certain reality or affect a certain goal. Often, when interacting with goal-oriented people, we perceive the clear message that they believe they can do whatever they want and that the actions that others take have no influence over their behaviors. They decide how things will go long before they find themselves in a situation and, thus, are closed off to any stimulus or inspiration, be it interior or exterior.

Predetermined and locked-in behaviors force all kinds of manipulations within us and toward others, making it impossible for the Truth of any moment to reveal itself fully. Any intention that wants to control another is, by nature, manipulative.

If we intend, for example, to "make the other feel bad" or even "to make them happy," we are already trying to control them, whereas if we select, for example, to "shine a light on the issue," we're not assuming their emotional state. Whether they feel bad or happy (or any other emotional by-product of our exchange), we understand it is beyond our control, and instead, we are able to give our energy to things we are responsible for and can influence. The imagery that comes to us intuitively, when we are not trying to manipulate ourselves, others, or the outcome, is so much more *creative, fun, dynamic, inventive,* and *expansive* that it really quite easily becomes an art form.

> *"The sculpture is already complete within the marble block before I start my work. It is already there; I just have to chisel away the superfluous material."*
>
> — MICHELANGELO BUONAROTTI

When discussing "The Prisoners" Michelangelo spoke of liberating the beings from within the marble he sculpted, he did not force a form into taking shape, he allowed it to be discovered, revealed, born in the moment, based on the materials at hand with respect for their unique expression, as he perceived it. There was no manipulation of the material for an end result, but rather an emancipation of what was within, that took place.

An active intention does not assume any physical or emotional state.

Instead of trying to induce an emotional or a physical state, which is out of our field of abilities, we want to expand our awareness of our Essential Nature, doing the work to nurture our Authentic Selves. Physicality and emotionality do not fully represent us, nor are they states we can pre-plan or take for granted, nor lean on for our feelings of *wholeness*. Our needs would be better served were we to remain available to our highest Inner Wisdom, independent of the circumstances, the people, the emotions, and physical realities that come and go over a lifetime.

For example, an active intention would not presuppose making someone feel tired, excited, bored, or worried, as physical and emotional states are not controllable. Nor would we assume ourselves to have to be in any certain state at any future time. Telling ourselves (or others) that we've got to be or feel a certain way is unproductive and cruel and ignores what *is* at any moment. It is unimaginative and untruthful and bores us into apathy. Just ask any actor given a line reading instead of being allowed to find the most *Truthful* expression within.

We do not pre-plan or even concern ourselves with such occupations because we immediately recognize misdirected energy use when we are fully present with active intentions grounded in our True Essence, which is the Highest *Goodness, Joy,* or *Love*.

The least imaginative director I've ever worked with, a well-known Florentine theater-maker, represents for me the death of creativity possible when we initiate expression from the ego's desire to dominate and control every aspect of any given moment. A few years back, he hired me for a production I hadn't auditioned for, and from the first rehearsal, I realized that his approach to theater-making was completely contrived, inauthentic, dishonest, and manipulative. And that is the consciousness from which he wrote, directed, produced, and acted; nothing unique or original could blossom. These are behaviors deeply rooted in the fear of incompetency, which I do not deny this individual; I merely invite self-emancipation from such rigidity for the Love and Glory of Creation.

An active intention is be-able.

Thanks to the goal-oriented nature of Western society, we may tend to believe that our happiness is found in *doing* something or other, as opposed to *being* something or another (preferably our Soulful Selves). The manner in which an active intention is manifested is to *be* it rather than to do it. To respond to Life with great intention is to be in a state of Consciousness that goes beyond the act of doing something. There is little to nothing actually to do and an Infinite Universe of options for what to embody.

When our intentions are clear and concise, concerning ourselves less with what or how we do and more with embodying the intention, we welcome an array of possibilities into scope, which facilitates the realization of the ideal outcome. Vibrating and interacting from a position of non-judgmental awareness enables our potential.

Everyone is Innately equipped for Being, proven through simple observation of our essence: we *are*.

For something to be physically capable of being done doesn't necessarily guarantee its effectiveness. Very little needs doing when our direct and concise intention is incorporated, integrated, and embodied. An empowered intention can, like a beacon in the dark, be invested in and embraced no matter what the physical conditions of the circumstance may appear to be. In this manner, we bring our *being*-ness into our *doing*-ness.

An active intention is fun.

An uncountable variety of intentions is possible in any particular Life scenario, though some may be more practical and productive than others. The important quality to weave into all of our intentions is our *"joie de vivre,"* our Joy of Life, a sense of curiosity, playfulness, and fun according to our heart's contentment.

What compels us? What does our Creative Genius wish to embody? What does our *wisdom* suggest to us as we ignite our sense of play? What pulls us to our highest, most sublime vibrational state? What intentions force us to engage with *light* in our hearts?

Let's choose words that excite us, using language as a doorway to our most vibrant, active, and courageous imagination, beyond what we would normally do, beyond what we've ever done or seen done. Envision yourself "giving a compliment" when admiring your best friend... Now envision yourself "crowning a queen/king" instead... Which is more *fun* for you? And which do you think would be more stimulating for you and your Life co-stars and collaborators?

"All the fun's in how you say a thing."

— ROBERT FROST

Superficiality simply doesn't suffice as a form of communication or a means of Creation. Our willingness to go deep, to enquire about what lies beyond our current perceptions, remaining in receptive silence requires strength of heart and courage. And once we get a feel for it, there is no going back to pretending we are materialistic or superficial Beings. Once we've sensed the profundity of our Essence, and that of every other sentient Being, our appreciation for Life, for all of Creation, runs equally as deep.

With the choice to fully be all that we came here to be, an awareness of prolific *abundance, joy,* and *limitless potential* shows up and is ours to embody. When we open ourselves to the depths of our Being, we access what is beyond the surface, beyond the daily, beyond errands, tasks, and distractions, to uncover what we cannot yet imagine.

Of course, there are times when a fairly mundane intention is perfectly applicable; "open the car door for grandma" is as simple as that, although I suggest the manner in which you open said door has vast creative possibilities. The idea is to find intention in what means something to you, what matters to you, what gets you going, what turns you on, what pulls you towards greater and grander expression; and only you know what that is; your Inner Wisdom contains that information, not your intellect.

> *"Creativity is an ode to life. It is not a form of entertainment. It is a form of joy."*
>
> — WYNN BULLOCK

The way we word our intentions and the tone in which we speak to ourselves is demonstrated in our actions. When we are clear, concise, specific, *joyful*, *playful*, and *loving* with our active intentions, our communication is as well. An intention brings us the feeling tone known as *joy*; its realization, its actual manifestation, uplifts us with a vibration of lightness and *illumination*. The completion of an intention merely reveals other opportunities for continual *creative expression*. As we are already *whole*; an intention which has run its course, perhaps even delivering an ideal outcome, cannot complete us. It can, however, energetically fuel our upward spiral of self-knowing toward an awareness of *blissful* well-being.

Doing what we intend

"Creative work is a gift to the world and every being in it. Don't cheat us of your contribution. Give us what you've got."

— Steven Pressfield

Infinite possibility abides within us all, and we are each equipped with everything we need to allow our lives to transform into an expression of our own unique Life Artistry. Our options for self-expression are *immeasurable*; we've countless abilities for actively living as our fullest potential. Once we know what our intention is in any given experience, we instinctively sense the impulse to take action, to **do** something. When we are led by the intellect, our finite mind makes suggestions based on what it has seen, heard of, experienced, or perceived in the past, and yes, a strong impulse to DO arises. When we are in-tune with our True Nature and aware that the possibilities are *Infinite*, our Inner Wisdom suggests an inspired variety of actions, behaviors, tones, vibrations, all in service of our intentions. Our Intuition speaks to us, providing us with information through our own inner communion and communication. The Life Artist within is listening, taking cues, direction, and guidance directly from your uniqueness, your ways, your Beingness, all that is actively expressing as you.

VERBS

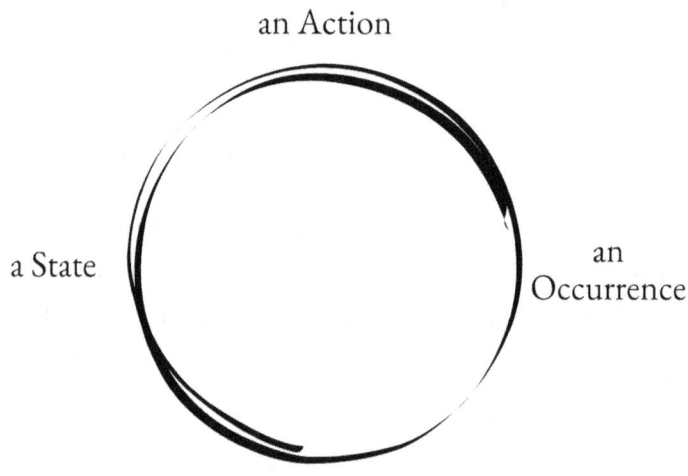

As vibrational-social Beings, we tend to grasp onto words to describe the language of our insights. When we use words to identify these suggestions, we know them grammatically as verbs: words used to describe an action, a state, or an occurrence. If my intention, for example, is towards "creating an understanding," my Intuition immediately brings a variety of "actions" to my awareness and suggestions on how to react or respond. Immediately, ideas arise such as invite, share, enlighten, build, accept, invent, acknowledge, confirm, detail, relax, and any other number of verbs. Whichever options I select remain to be determined in the instant they arise as possibilities; thus, I permit myself to make those decisions in the moment and authentically. Creating a skill for identifying what I do and what others do through non-judgmental observance not only helps me know myself better, it encourages me to expand my possibilities of behavior.

Unleash The Verbs : Name your behaviors game.

There are literally thousands of words to describe your actions, your state, and your experiences. For this exercise, you'll focus on *verbs*, as to identify your behaviors. Once you become aware of your preferred verbs through making a Conscious list of your most commonly practiced actions, you can expand the options through playful experimentation. Let's take a deeper look at your verbs.

Ask yourself: Am I exploring and encouraging new, uplifting, fun, generous, loving behaviors that mean something to me and have the qualities of Life I am organically drawn to?

Most of us stick with the same old collection of habitual behaviors we've memorized over the years that have either worked to get us what we want or have been previously established as part of our "personality."

Beyond the obvious Life activities of, say, sleeping, eating, digesting, evacuating, thinking, reading, sitting, walking, talking, cooking, washing, driving, etc., what do you do in your daily Life, from moment to moment?

For example, right now, you are sitting, standing, or reclining, reading, breathing, blinking, and may even be digesting. And what else are you doing?

Expand your awareness and imagination: Are you receiving, playing, opening, releasing, studying, observing, listening, celebrating, expanding, learning, growing, challenging, contemplating, registering, or engaging in any other behavior?

Do these activities bore, stimulate, provoke, encourage, entertain, motivate, or any other number of states within you?

What is happening right now during this occurrence: is it reassuring, teasing, inviting, blaming, criticizing, inspiring, or embracing you?

Deepen your awareness around your actions and choices with this fun exercise of naming what you are doing at any given moment and as you go through your day.

Make a list in your journal or even in your mind*. Take notice as you surprise and delight yourself with not only what you do but also with the wonderful new suggestions that arise after the obvious is identified.

Once you are aware of your usual collection of already mastered and well-practiced (quasi-automatic) activities and find your Creative Genius familiar with, yet uninterested in the predictability being revealed, unleash your wild imagination and go on a treasure hunt for new options!

Notice how beautifully inspiration appears in moments you never would have expected had you not intentionally ignited your skills for observation and your curiosity for possibility. Feel your gaze opening to include the entire human experience and enjoy the glory that comes when you embody your Innate Creativity.

---

* I recommend you start this exploration with a journal so that you can make a comprehensive and complete list of your daily behaviors. Seeing your most practiced verbs on paper allows for a vast opening in your imagination once you begin to look outside of the normal patterns of practiced actions, states, and occurrences. Soon, your verb-awareness will expand, and you'll find yourself enjoying this practice even without pen & paper.

> *"Don't be too timid and squeamish about your actions. All life is an experiment. The more experiments you make, the better."*
>
> — RALPH WALDO EMERSON

Being what we intend

Now, let's develop our awareness beyond what we do and towards what we *are*; in essence, we're looking to embody our intentions as opposed to projecting or demonstrating them, in other words, 'being' instead of 'doing' something.

Take a look at your active verbs list. These are words that contain an action, and when we are in integrity with our True Nature and aligned with our innate Creative Genius, they embody both physical and energetic components.

Pick one from these words that mean something to you personally, representing how you may behave or act when communicating successfully.

Ask yourself: May I transform this word into a State of Being?

Example: *If the active verb is to inspire... I could be inspired, or I could embody Inspiration, itself.*

What does that expression bring forth in me? What are the energetic qualities of inspiration within me?

When I meditate on the fullness of Life contained in the invitation to "embody inspiration," the insights begin to emerge, ranging from inhaling to enlightening, from uplifting to inciting, etc.

Example*: If the verb is to teach... I could be in a state of embodying precisely the wisdom I am teaching; I could also be taught or teachable.*

What does that expression feel and look like? What is that posture? That tone and timing? That dynamic?

When I meditate on the fullness of Life contained in the invitation to "embody the wisdom I am teaching," the insight that emerges is quite simply: Embracing Brilliance by being the Creatively Genius Life Artist I am, entirely. This is a Spiritual Practice in my daily Life, and can be in yours as well.

Explore the possibility of transforming your actions into States of Being and play with being them! Notice how easily embodiment manifests in creative expressions that are meaningful to you.

When I have an intention, for example, "to facilitate a connection," I can embody or be the expression of that intention. I don't have to *do* anything to facilitate a connection because I am already interconnected with All of Life; instead, I get to *be* the frequency of what I already am, of what I choose to experience, and of how I prefer to communicate. I cannot control those with whom I interact, and I would never aim to manipulate others or myself; I can, however, be the thing I hope to experience. I can be what I choose to create: I can be the essence of connectedness in order to encourage a sense of connection with myself and others.

In a poignant chapter of my life, a new client reached a harrowing point of despair, contemplating suicide. As I positioned myself in Consciousness as their Spiritual Guide, the gravity of the situation demanded a compassionate enrichment of my State of Being. The fundamental intention of embodying a State of Consciousness transformed into *facilitating a connection*. For, at the core of this individual's suffering was their deep-rooted conviction of being separate and alone, with themes of abandonment and isolation regularly showing up and playing out in her experiences.

In the crucible of that moment, embodying the intention became paramount. It meant relinquishing preconceived notions that may have inadvertently crept in and relinquishing any trace of opinion or judgment, as well as any need to "fix" or to "heal". My presence was invited to transcend mere words and actions; this service required a profound willingness to *be* the intention rather than to simply execute it.

This shift led to transformative behaviors. Instead of offering advice, I embraced, loved, and comforted, with an intensity born of genuine inner-standing. The intention "to facilitate a connection" opened the door to a new realm of empathy and self-compassion within her. We communed in a space where I was able to embody uplifting inspiration, not through lofty words but through a sincere and authentic connectedness. Soon, she experienced what some would call a miraculous healing in that a massive shift in her perceptions occurred. She began seeing her inseparability with All of Life, thus realizing that many of the events she'd encountered were pathways to the remembrance of her True Nature as a *whole, integral* and *beloved* expression of the One Living Organism within which her Being resides, just as It lives and breathes in her, as her. A new outlook on Life transformed her autobiography title from "Alone" to its original state of "All One."

My responsibility lay in my willingness to be present, embodying the incarnation of my intention, which innately contained the qualities of *wholeness* and *love*. In that vulnerability, I discovered a strength that transcended the conventional boundaries of relationships. Through this intentional connection, I became a source of solace and hope, illustrating the multi-faceted impact of embodying an intention rather than doing an intention. The experience left an indelible mark on us both, emphasizing the efficacy and potency of presence and the transformative potential that lives within a genuine intention. That individual allowed themselves to experience a 180° change of perspective on Life and their connection with It. Compassion now guides their days and ways; their State of Being is peaceful, trusting, and empowered.

Take it to Another Level: Name your States of Being

Revisit your verbs list and expand it into an awareness of various States of Being. Play around with embodying the behaviors as energetic frequencies. Instead of doing the behaviors, commit to embody them, be them.

Move around, speak and express yourself as that behavior as fully and entirely as you possibly can with your entire self. Commit to it, invite your playful nature to experiment with it, to have fun being it.

Explore various intentions, try them on and see how they sound, move, and feel, in your Being.

Enjoy noting the specifics of different intentions and how they inform and influence your choices and behaviors.

Take special notice of how your breathing and heart rate change to suit your State of Being.

Set an intention for a communication in your near future, and before that exchange, practice a few verb options in relation to that intention. Recognize those behaviors and actions as Vibrational Frequencies and allow yourself to fully embody them as States of Being, as a practice of self-tuning to their Essence. Don't pre-plan your behaviors, but instead select a State of Being that feels dynamic, open, intelligent, authentic, loving, truthful to your intention.

Once in the actual communication:

Remind yourself of your intention, and be aware of how willing you are to commit to expressing and conveying that intention.

Note if you allow the real-life circumstances to hinder you from committing fully to your intention. Notice if habitual identity-preserving blockages arise to "protect" you and be aware of your willingness to move beyond what is familiar.

Compassionately observe how fully you are listening to the other(s) and to your inner guidance, how flexible you are, and how available you are towards adaptation while in communication.

My dad has shared much wisdom with me. In fact, we love sharing insights and realizations based on our mutual curiosity about the human condition. One of the countless jewels he has repeated to me over the years is the suggestion that "Flexibility is a sign of *intelligence*" in people. In other words, our willingness to adapt is a reflection of our Innate Genius. I couldn't agree more, as I have witnessed in my own Life and in the Lives of my students, clients, friends, and loved ones, the utter simplicity and truthfulness of this philosophy.

Being willing to change, grow, and adapt in any given moment is part of our Inherent Intelligence. Especially in scenarios of high importance, when our unconscious habit of avoiding change often kicks in, we are extremely well-served in nurturing our *natural* talent of adaptability. All of Nature is in a state of incessant change; the only absolute in Life is Life Itself, which will continue into Eternity, regardless of whether or not we are here to watch it. Flexibility, being willing to bend, as opposed to break, allows for resilience and adaptability in the face of Life's unpredictable (yet guaranteed) twists and turns.

"Nothing is softer or more flexible than water, yet nothing can resist it."

— Lao Tzu

And So, It Is

"Everybody born comes from the Creator trailing wisps of glory. We come from the Creator with creativity. I think that each one of us is born with creativity."

— Maya Angelou

Once we comprehend the current circumstance we find ourselves within by identifying what is perceived to be occurring, and we locate the vital active intention of our communication, we're ready to fully embody our expression of it. Intention is a great, powerful tool, and its exploration encourages us to expand our creativity.

For a future, consciously communicative experience, I can facilitate a higher outcome through visioning, affirmative statements, and active meditation. By "higher outcome," I intend to mean an experience of the frequencies of the highest level of Consciousness I allow myself at any given moment. My effectiveness is influenced by my commitment to my intentions. Practice, in the initial phase of awakening to any new awareness, can be quite fruitful and useful for opening one's perspective and facilitating creativity. Creation is Consciousness to its fullest potential; thus, consciously exploring intentionality with openness, curiosity, playfulness, and availability to the possibilities is of useful practice.

Just as the fledgling pianist must devote their attention to mastering "chopsticks" to develop coordination and a sense of timing, and the burgeoning illustrator must, with equal fervor, dedicate their energy to sketching to nurture confidence and sharpen problem-solving skills, the emerging Life Artist is encouraged to direct their vital Life-force towards practiced embodiment. All artists know that devoted practice is the path to *creative freedom*. The key to a successful practice is our willingness to be alert and present throughout, to never allow mindless repetition to hijack our craft, but rather to remain playfully interactive as if each session were occurring for the very first time.

Activating the imagination, inviting the right brain to contribute to our Conscious realization, we can access an energetic playground for our development. Because the left brain has been trained to follow logical/limited and analytical information from a decisive perspective, we return to our natural gifts for assistance. Our imagination, not our memory, nor even our projections on the future, but our activated imagination in the present moment, is the bridge connecting logic with *infinite* possibility. We take our comprehension of the experience, morphing that into a clear and active intention... and with that awareness, with that understanding, we liberate our "knowing" mind for something wondrous beyond our initial perception.

"Imagination is the beginning of creation. You imagine what you desire, you will what you imagine, and at last, you create what you will."

— GEORGE BERNARD SHAW

It wasn't until I was an adult that I received the prognosis that I was born with naturally balanced cognitive perception, which illuminated my understanding of why decision-making had emerged as a unique challenge in my early life. Blessed with the ability to see multiple facets of any topic, I could effortlessly imagine and comprehend diverse perspectives. While this cognitive *balance* allowed me a rich understanding, it posed a conundrum when it came to making choices, particularly those that required picking sides. This predicament often frustrated friends who urged me to take a stance and remain there forever. The insistence on choosing sides clashed with my Inherent cognitive *harmony*, causing tension between my *natural* inclination and societal expectations. The struggle was real, but it sparked a *beautiful* transformation in my approach to decision-making. Over time, I learned to integrate the *immeasurable intelligence* of my deeply compassionate heart.

In the evolution of my decision-making process, I shifted away from relying solely on mental calculations. The learned behavior of permitting only one neurological center to inform me became outdated. Instead, I embraced a holistic approach where my heart and gut played integral roles in any contemplation. This synthesis of cognitive *balance*, heart *coherence*, and emotional *intelligence* ushered a new era, making choices not only an intellectual exercise but a *harmonious* collaboration of mind, heart, and intuition.

Nowadays, decisions are a playful, co-creative dance between the intellectual and the mystical, a fluid integration that honors the complexity of my human experience. This journey has not only eased the challenges posed by the binary, finite mind, it has enriched my life with a deeper understanding of and connection with the *wisdom* that resides within us all.

> *"Even indecision is a decision; making no choice is still a choice."*
>
> — Chris Norton

We are able to bring about changes in our neurological wiring. We are able to rewrite our mental habits, given our willingness and devotion to transform so. Cognitive *balance*, so as not to be dominated by one lobe or the other, is available to those in the position to seek out such technologies. In mental *peace*, we then move from the neurological hub we call the brain down into the neurological, energetic hub we call the heart-center, where compassion resides. Heart and mind coherence is another possibility available to anyone willing to choose to experience it. There are innumerable meditations and breath exercises to explore, one of which is the simple, daily practice of self-compassion.

Practicing Self-Compassion

You can do this practice anytime you need a little self-compassion.

I find it most accessible when I am actually in the midst of a difficult situation. Perhaps stress is rising, I'm experiencing a relationship issue, or I am aware that a sense of worry is present.

As soon as you "hear" or feel the call for compassion, often echoed through the valley of judgment occurring within, begin by resting a hand on your chest plate, a.k.a. your heart-center.

Take a slow, conscious, full breath in and out as you turn your attention inwardly.

Acknowledge the difficulty by saying something like, "This is a call for compassion," or even "This moment is difficult for me."

Recognize the common humanity in the perception of suffering by saying something like, "Life is full of opportunities to love me" or even "I am profoundly identified with my suffering."

Finally, express loving kindness by saying something like, "May I be kind to myself in this moment" or even "I accept myself as I am right now."

Feel the warmth of your palm against your heart-center, as you use comforting language, just as you would with a dear friend, by saying something like, "There, there, my darling, I am with you" or even "I love you, you are safe".

Let go of the words, allowing yourself to just be, and remain in the silence as you observe your bodily sensations.

Compassion is our ability to understand what we are or what another is experiencing. If the future version of you could be imagined as someone other than you, perhaps "she," "he," or "they" could be someone with whom you create a compassionate connection. Can you imagine what that person (future you) would feel in a given circumstance? Of course you can because your experienced-based memories feed you with all kinds of data to justify any number of behaviors or feelings. And beyond that personal association with your future self, could you imagine, right now, a larger, more expansive, and all-trusting Being who, given any circumstance, is capable of compassionately embodying their *unique* version of *greatness, magnificence, beauty,* and *brilliance*? Of course you can because your True Essence is nothing short of Genius. And no life-event or person can rob you of what is Inherently you and yours.

> *"I would like my life to be a statement of love and compassion, and where it isn't, that's where my work lies."*
>
> — RAM DASS

The potential I express is only limited by my beliefs around my own limitations. I have lost count of the times I have doubted my abilities, doubted my potential, doubted my validity, my lovability, and my worthiness. The price for such beliefs is too high for my True Self to pay, for deep within me is a rebellious Soul that doesn't accept my perceived limitations and bucks back in the most *creative* ways when I slip into old habits. Completely accepting that all that is conceivable, is possible, I get to move forward from there. I'm not accepting the assignment of figuring out **how** the conceivable is possible. Instead, I am surrendering to the ageless *wisdom* that once a seed is planted, given the proper environment, it will come to fruition.

What my mind suggests "should" or "should not" be is a misuse of thought energy. Beyond those musings, something *exquisite* wants to emerge within and through me. I am fully able to respond to a progressive Life that is for me and never against me. I alone am responsible for recognizing and nourishing my innate Greatness.

There are limits to thought, however, for as I first began to see my True Nature, I noticed thought was still a constant chattering companion; my talkative intellect didn't stop offering guidance and input. And that's when it hit me: I don't want my mind to cease, for that would mean brain death! The nature of the mind is incessant thought. I am not here to control my thoughts, to contain or limit my mind beyond its inherent limitations; I am not even interested in quieting the mind, for that occurs organically whenever my Whole Being is in alignment.

Encountering new positions in Consciousness, I am self-empowered to explore various practices. When the Truth reveals itself to me, when it is upon me and I am steeped in it, I can feel it and recognize it as such, just like you can, for because it has a very specific energetic code of its own, we know the Truth by how it feels. It may take practice to identify the frequency of Truth within our Being, especially if we were taught to defer to others for our psychological or physical safety. However, I encourage us all to make the slight effort to gain familiarity with the quality of Truth and its felt Essence within us, the profundity and velocity of which may surprise and delight us. (For we really truly know the Truth by how it feels!) Once we've set our Inner Guidance System to "Truth Mode," we are immediately empowered to release techniques, modalities, and practices. Self-realized, we may simply be what we already are, all that we are fully; in other words, we are able to embrace our own unique expression of Creative Genius within.

Thus, trusting in Life, we take on our response-ability fearlessly, aware that only we can access our inherent wellness, *peace*, *joy*, and everlasting *happiness*. We become able to respond to Life from a place of *lovingness* and real self-recognition. This sense of *creative freedom* is what we are willingly giving ourselves over to. A surrender, a yielding begins to occur where, more than ever, our innate curiosity and *playful* nature invite us to further embody what's being revealed.

> *"The function of art is to do more than tell it like it is – it is to imagine what is possible."*
>
> — BELL HOOKS

Science now knows that the body has three neurological centers, not just the brain in the skull, but also the brain within the chest cavity (also known as the heart), and the brain within the lower torso (also known as the abdomen or the gut). When we call them "neurological centers," what we mean is that they're related to the nervous system, to our nerves and how they function in our anatomy, and how we function. One of my absolute favorite practices is the unification of the three primary energy centers of my Being. I love to share this practice as a guided meditation, and I suggest that if you'd like to explore it as such, you either record yourself reading it through so that you may listen to it in meditative practice or go to the following link to access a recording of it: https://youtu.be/E1jFqTW9gEw

---

The 3 Energy Centers Practice

I invite you now to find yourself in a comfortable position and do a quick body scan to make sure that your spine is in alignment so that your breath, blood, and energy can flow unhindered and with ease. If you'd like, you can rest your hands in your lap, palms facing upwards, or wherever they naturally fall on your thighs.

Gently close your eyes and take a moment to set an intention for this practice: for example, the embodiment of the quality of INTEGRITY, allowing stillness, tranquility, and a sense of wholeness into your body.

Direct your awareness first toward your belly, also known as the core, the gut area, or the abdomen. Direct your attention to that energy center and allow your inner awareness to be a sort of soothing balm. Let your belly relax, go round, and soften.

Place the palm of one of your hands on your relaxed belly. Be aware of how your breathing responds to your abdomen and how, when your belly area is softened, it influences your breathing. With your awareness directed to that part of your lower torso, the belly area, and lower back, become more acutely aware of the space you know as your core.

Begin to notice that this energy center is filled with its own Essence, its own self. And so, begin to notice the quality of the energy of the Core, your Core, your belly, your gut, without any opinions or judgments about it. You're simply observing the quality of that particular neurological center, allowing it to feel spacious and wide and open, noticing that this energy center actually does go beyond the physical body and into the subtle body, beyond form. Allow your awareness to be like a loving caress.

Recognizing that the energy centers that make up the first three chakras are all related to your humanness and to your survival, understand that the gut, core, and belly energy center is where not only your emotional Life exists but also where your corporeal life exists. It's where you get nutrition, it's where you process, it's where you create, it's where you release and evacuate, it's also where your human relationships and your social relationships find their reference.

Take a sweet, soothing breath in, inhaling Integrity and exhale, releasing any old beliefs you may carry about the wisdom of your core energy center.

Lifting that awareness now to the heart center, the chest region, the upper torso, and observe how your breath is in relation to this particular neurological center. And allow the chest, the heart, the lower and the upper lungs, and even the upper back to be made of space. If you please, you may rest the palm of your other hand on your chest area.

Go beyond form and even become aware that there's no content here, that there's an energy that is densified as this heart center. This energy center has its own Essence within you. Now, notice the quality of that energy center there. Your heart intentionally breathes spaciousness into it. Notice that its Essence, its energy, and its qualities go beyond the physical and move into the subtle body, which is beyond form. Notice how your awareness is like a spotlight on these beautiful qualities contained energetically within you.

Your awareness is gently resting on your heart-center. Referencing this energy center, this neurological center, because here's where your awareness of being a multidimensional individual comes into play. The heart-center is also known as the seat of the Soul. Compassion and love are said to reside here, as well as your ability to serve, your willingness to embody generosity, and the Givingness of Source. All this and more originates in this celebrated center. The heart-center is also where you receive, allow and surrender.

Take a sweet, soothing breath in, inhaling Integrity and exhale, releasing any old beliefs you may carry about the wisdom of your heart energy center.

And I invite you once again to lift your awareness, this time to your head, crown energy center, and breathe. Do a full inhalation and exhalation as if you could fill that area with air. And in doing so, allow yourself the awareness that there's space here in the crown, skull, head.

More than content, there's energy here, and it has its own quality, unique, different from the heart, and different from the core. Observe the quality of your head energy center, crown energy center, noticing that its vibration, its energetic quality actually goes beyond your skull, goes beyond the physical; breathe spaciousness into that energy center. Simply be with the awareness that also this energy center goes beyond form. You're observing its quality with no opinions, no judgment about it, just witnessing.

Gently resting your awareness on the crown center, understand that this neurological center is where the binary yes/no, right/wrong thinking is said to reside. It's also where your memories are stored, as well as the things you document and measure in life.

Take a sweet, soothing breath in, inhaling Integrity and exhale, releasing any old beliefs you may carry about the wisdom of your crown energy center.

You are now uniting these three brains or three neurological centers in the body; that's the gut or the Core, the heart, and the crown of the head. Imagine joining the Intelligence of your Core with your heart and your crown; feel the union of your Intuition, your compassion, and your Intelligence. See a rod of light connecting your belly, your heart center, and your mind. This is an act of Self-alignment and energetic elevating, a celebration of all that is encapsulated in your Whole Being, even beyond the limits of form.

Embrace the profound unity of your gut, heart, and crown by gently joining your palms in front of your heart center. A subtle bow of your head symbolizes gratitude and self-recognition, acknowledging the perfectly integrated individual within - the Sacred and Holy Being that is you. Recognize the elevated one, a manifestation of harmony and wholeness, as the Life Artist within you. The inner Creative Genius is alive in and as your very Existence. Enjoy the fruits of this divine inner connection. Feel free to extend this practice in a way that is meaningful to you.

THE "ACT AS IF" PRINCIPLE

Acting "as if" is an easily applicable technique used for inspiring motivation and liberating new levels of response-ability through conscious embodiment. In the realm of psychology, it's acknowledged as one of the simplest forms of non-trance, positive self-hypnosis. It is a cognitive behavioral strategy that ignites a powerful magnetic energy, allowing us to tap into and collaborate with the Law of Assumption. The practice is a simple process of behaving *As If* something were happening in a positive manner.

Doubt will arise to contradict even the suggestion that things might go well, so if that is the response showing up within your awareness right now, forgive yourself, let a smile turn the corners of your mouth upwardly, and realize that we're onto something big that is sparking a memorized protection response that is ready to be released. By adopting the posture, vibrational tone, and physical essence of ourselves in an unfolding positive experience, we access a deeper flow of inner *wisdom*. While maintaining the exercise of fully investing in our intention within an imagined reality, we source new responses to Life. The Laws of Assumption, Allowance, Attraction, and Actualization play off one another while simultaneously enriching our relationship with the quality of *trust*.

In moments when I've struggled with low self-esteem, high anxiety levels, depression, or lack of motivation, the *creative* principle of acting "as if" has generated confidence and courage. I often apply this practice as a way of energizing self-realization and fueling inevitable action. Behaving "as if" I actively intend something very specific, allowing the behaviors, movements, expressions, tones, vocabulary, posture, pace, volume, and all manners of being to become my own, I willingly embody the feelings associated with that intention's successful fulfillment. The body cannot decipher the difference between a real or an imagined experience. Thus, the feelings, impulses, and flashes of insight will all be *unique* to me and *true* to my current place in Consciousness.

> *"As someone thinks within himself, so he is."*
>
> — PROVERBS 23:7

In its simplest form, this self-suggestion exercise is a matter of imagining yourself as *being* that which you choose to experience, imagining the possibility of being delighted, fulfilled, or excited about a hypothetical positive experience, the exploration and practice of which facilitates our trading fear or anxiety for self-esteem, trust, and confidence. If you are nervous about a certain meeting or conversation, acting "as if" beforehand can build social courage and a sense of preparedness. Professionals in dangerous or unpredictable work environments use this technique to manage nerves and deal with their sense of vulnerability. Despite feeling otherwise, they appear calm, cool, and collected in the face of the unknown. This is NOT the old adage, "Fake it until you make it," for there is no need for faking anything; this practice, when done earnestly, brings about pure authenticity and a raw, exhilarating vulnerability the ego will quickly hide from, suggesting you "fake it" as to keep you "safe" from the unknown contained within *Infinite* possibilities.

In my personal journey, I've found immense value in embracing the "as if" technology, a fundamental practice I learned as a young actor and speaker, as a form of preparation for performance. The practice goes beyond mere rehearsal; it's a transformative exploration that provides an opportunity to inquire into and experience my Natural instincts, reactions, responses, and intuitions. It develops my willingness to improvise, strengthens my observational skills, and expands my range of possibilities. From a position of *wholeness* and in no physical, emotional, or psychological danger whatsoever, I get to investigate potentiality, consequences, importance, outcomes, and detachment. As a *creative* exercise, it fortifies my playfulness, inviting my childlike, inquisitive Nature to come join the fun, which is essential to my Creative Self-liberation, freeing and empowering the Life Artist I am. Beyond its theatrical applicability, acting "as if" has become a powerful tool in my skill-set.

I have vividly and actively applied this practice in so-called real Life on countless occasions. Recently, in the midst of a serious health crisis involving my Dad, I encountered situations where I was called to embody a sense of confidence and resilience beyond what I felt capable of. Channeling the "Act As If" approach, I embodied the energetic reality of a composed, self-assured, and tranquil individual despite internal uncertainties. The practice not only helped me navigate the challenges that presented themselves with *grace*, as opposed to fear, arrogance, or defensiveness (which would not have helped me or Dad at all), but also provided me with insights into my own *unique creative* responses to Life. This practice was felt by everyone with whom I came into contact, Dad included, raising the energetic frequency of all involved: family members, neighbors, technicians, nurses, and physicians. It is a miraculous, powerful practice that I encourage you to explore within your own Life events.

An "as if" is a suggestive device used to assess what a particular experience means to you energetically. It is a lively, compelling, simple, and acceptable fantasy within which your imagination is free to create. It is something that potentially could happen that you can accept unequivocally and respond to immediately. An "as if" imagining is described in as few words as possible, ideally, no more than one sentence in length, so as to be easily accessible for reference when exploring its energetic qualities. An "as if" contains enough details to activate the imagination but not so many as to form a decisive narrative. It sparks imagination, which fuels investment in fantasy; it is not a substitute for reality; it is a device created to incite inventiveness by personalizing our intentions.

When used well, the application of an "as if" will distance us from the story we are telling ourselves, opening a space where we can access connections and new responses particular to our intentions and inspired preferences.

The As If Foundation

Name a circumstance in your Life where you have intentions.

In relation to that circumstance, choose an intention that turns your nervous system on, that brings excitement to your body, and ideas to your imagination. Select one of the dozens of intentions you could have in a day and bring it to the front of your mind. Make it into a simple, clear phrase with as few words as possible.

What follows is an example of the application of an "as if." See if you can use your chosen intention to implement the practice of imagining an "as if" as you understand this model.

CIRCUMSTANCE: You're at work speaking with a colleague about a new project you are developing.

INTENTION: Your ideal outcome is seeing them volunteer to support you by joining your team. Your active intention is: *to inspire greatness* in your colleague.

Now, with that active intention in mind, invent a completely hypothetical scenario that mirrors the level of importance and the energetic qualities of this intention. Remember to consciously make this made-up scenario completely <u>hypothetical</u>, as in, it has never happened, it will likely never happen, but if it did, you would feel, behave, and respond in ways that mirror the active intention of *inspiring greatness*.

AS IF: *To inspire greatness...* It is AS IF you are getting your adult cousin, who is very cautious by nature, to jump from a cliff into the sea, twenty feet below, where you await her.

She can swim and loves water, but you can imagine that this could feel like a minor risk for her. You know she is in no danger, and you already sense that you can embody many behaviors (verbs) to get her to throw herself freely into the water.

In imagining this hypothetical situation, you can immediately sense the vast options available to you while communicating with her.

Allow your body to begin experimenting, playing with and enjoying various states of being that would contribute to enlisting support by *inspiring greatness*, in the form of her jumping off the cliff.

As soon as it is evident that your body and mind can invest in this hypothetical scenario, you are free to play!

"See" the situation and yourself in it.

There are thousands of ways to *inspire greatness*. What would you do? Who would you be? In what ways would you communicate if this were the truth of your present experience? How far would you go to inspire?

Start to act as if this situation, this context, is really occurring... how would you resonate with your cousin? What would your body do? How would your voice sound? And if that didn't work... how would you change tone, vocabulary, behavior, embodiment? And if that didn't work?

Keep in mind there is no right or wrong way of approaching an imaginary scenario, there are simply embodiments that function and embodiments that do not function, in service of your ideal outcome and active intention. Set yourself free to really experiment and play with possible behaviors on your part.

If the stakes are high for your real-life situation, if it is important for you to "inspire greatness from colleagues" for a project you love, you will invest and you will uncover all kinds of new ways of being, of bringing your intentions to Life!

Instead of investing in the emotional and mental preoccupations or anxieties towards an experience, we can choose to create an imaginary personal investment in our chosen active intention for that experience. In this exercise, we connect to our intention by imbuing it with meaning.

In applying this technique, we are encouraged to be more than we currently imagine ourselves as. The process of being active with intention facilitates a natural endorphin release, which leads to better health and wellness, and feelings of ability, possibility, joy and inspiration.

The As If Exercise (for daily practice)

Your future self is pulling you towards your True Nature. Project any given circumstance, location, Living Being, and subject (context) into your imagination.

Imagine a real-life circumstance, in your mind's eye, "see" where you are, with whom you are interacting, and what is at hand.

Where are you, with whom are you interacting, and about what?

CIRCUMSTANCE: I am at a doctor's office with a physician and my Dad speaking about his health.

Now focus on your desired Highest outcome and locate your purest, most active intention.

Example: My ideal outcome is to get a plan of action that suits Dad's needs and involves the physician. I want the doctor to profoundly invest in Dad's care.

INTENTION: My intention is *to get a commitment.*

Now, based on your intention, create an imaginary, hypothetical situation that has never happened and will likely never happen, but if it did, you would feel, behave, and respond in ways that mirror the active intention.

AS IF: I am on the phone with my siblings discussing a family reunion.

Say out loud: *It's as if I am on the phone discussing a family reunion with my siblings.*

My intention is to get a commitment.

Repeat your active intention in your mind. Say the words to yourself as you breathe.

To get a commitment.

Now, come to the realization that your intention has sparked new possibilities.

See the imagined experience from a position of wholeness, lovingness, acceptance, fulfillment, or "success" (as you define it).

Imagine your (usually resistant) sibling accepting the idea and committing to bringing the event to fruition. Feel what that means to you.

Embody your greatness fully. Breathe, move, and speak as if you Truly are everything you intend to be.

Who would you be if you were in the process of getting this commitment?

What would be the quality of your behaviors, tone, and vocabulary?

In what ways, out of infinite options, would you interact with your siblings?

As you embody the intention, begin to feel the verb *to commit*.

What is the unique energetic reality of that active word: *commit*?

What is the one-of-a-kind vibration of *commitment*?

Become aware of these new postures, impulses, and vibrations. Feel your infinite potential manifested. Are you *committed*?

What Inner Wisdom arises as you allow the Essence

of your intention to express through your very Life and Being?

Dedicate some space right now to feel into the possibilities of getting a commitment.

It is *as if* your intention has been not only fully realized but that other manifestations reaching way beyond have now come into the realm of possibility.

And so, it is.

Now that you've felt it, you are aware of it as an entrance into your greatest glory. You can use this exercise as a gateway to unlimited creative potential.

"A man paints with his brains and not with his hands."

— Michelangelo Buonarotti

The Law of Allowance emphasizes the importance of consent in the process of manifestation. This principle encourages an unfaltering expectation that a desired outcome is in the process of unfolding, which mustn't be contradicted with any negating thoughts of doubt about said materialization. The absence of the desired demonstration is believed to be rooted in conflicting, often hidden, beliefs about the material outcome of a desire. From my experience, I understand it as a clear communication from an Intelligence beyond my own that something Greater is seeking expression through me. I am being invited to surrender.

At a heightened position in Consciousness, accessed through Spiritual practices, somatic movement, sacred study, breathwork, prayer, and meditation, we move away from intellectualization, and away from mental projections. In a state of gratitude, no request is being made. Through surrender, there is the release of attachment to the outcome. At that stage in our process of Inner realization, our vision changes. Willingness replaces willfulness. Our receptivity expands, our awareness increases, and acceptance is fully felt and given sans judgment. Outcome ceases to be our focus, and instead, we are fully invested in the endlessly blossoming Now, where all potential and All of Life exists.

Occurrences become revelations when we are able to respond to Life as it unfolds in the present moment. We learn to surrender to what is revealed, to the unknown, wisely trusting that we already are who we need to be to evolve into the next phase of our journey toward self-realization. Recognizing that our inner evolution is by no means a linear experience, we gain intimacy with more complex geometries. We embrace the *unknown*, where *immeasurable* possibilities reside, with *pure* appreciation for its gifts. As we enhance these Life-affirming aspects, our minds open, our hearts are invigorated, and our Consciousness is enlivened, accelerating inspiration and courageously welcoming the *infinite unknown* into our awareness.

"Letting there be room for not knowing is the most important thing of all. When there's a big disappointment, we don't know if that's the end of the story. It may just be the beginning of a great adventure. Life is like that. We don't know anything. We call something bad; we call it good. But really, we just don't know."

— Pema Chödrön

The Courage to Surrender

"Courage is falling in love with the unknown."

— Osho

The secret key to our wildest dreams becoming reality, to our greatest successes and our most *beautiful* expressions, is through the act of surrender. Communion with our *glorious* self, with our *Divine Nature* and its *creativity*, with those around us and with all sentient Beings, is the path to our grandest, most empowered, most *Truthful Essence*.

In the midst of life's ever-evolving tapestry, there was a moment of profound surrender that etched itself into the very fabric of my existence. It was a time of great internal suffering when the weight of expectations, personal aspirations, and the ceaseless pursuit of control had me ensnared. The struggle seemed interminable, and my heart yearned for release.

Amidst the clamor, a decisive Inner Wisdom arose, gently whispering, "Surrender is not giving up; it is letting go to something greater." Intrigued yet hesitant, I decided to test the waters of surrender. I relinquished the chokehold on my plans, fears, and desires, allowing the current of Life to guide me. This pivotal moment arrived during a career transition, a transformative experience that carried many unknowns with it. Contradictory to my Protective Personality's wishes, instead of meticulously plotting each step, I chose to embrace the uncertainty with an open heart. I surrendered the need for a predefined outcome and allowed Spirit to orchestrate its symphony around and for me.

> *"Art is a collaboration between God and the artist, and the less the artist does, the better."*
>
> — ANDRE GIDE

An unforeseen opportunity arose as I let go of the illusion of control. It was an invitation to immerse myself in a project that resonated with my deepest self. The surrender opened doors that my strategic planning never could have imagined. In that surrender, I found liberation. The shackles of self-imposed constraints and limitations melted away, and I was *free* to dance with the rhythm of the Cosmos. The journey became a vivid exploration of trust, intuition, and Divine alignment.

Empowered by surrender, I discovered a richer essence of Existence, a deeper quality of Life. Each day became a canvas, painted with the hues of newfound *joy*, purpose, and serendipity. The Universe, it seemed, was conspiring to manifest my *Highest Good*.

This sacred act of surrender became a gateway to greater Consciousness. It wasn't a defeat but a triumphant emergence into a realm where the Interconnectedness of All that Is became palpable. In surrendering, I found strength, and in letting go, I discovered the *boundless* nature of my own Being.

> *"The moment of surrender is not when life is over. It's when it begins."*
>
> — Marianne Williamson

The universal Law of Radiance is evident when an insight, born from our core *wisdom*, emanates. A *brilliance* so *unique* can only be the fruit of allowance, willingness, acceptance, and surrender. What a shift in perspective it was to understand that in order to awaken to my *Greatest Good*, I actually had to be willing to allow and make space for it. Emergence became a way of *Life*, a healing and *luminous* vibrational cord that brings me such wellness I forget all physical laws of manifestation and mentation, heading instead for the much more *blissful* state of awareness that comes with yielding to the Law of Love that creates, sustains, and maintains All That Is.

> *"It is through art, and through art only, that we can realize our perfection."*
>
> — OSCAR WILDE

There is an emergence occurring right now. In this field of *Infinite* possibilities and *Infinite* potential, you are already *complete, perfect,* and *whole*. How delightful it is to witness the profound relief on people's faces when they hear the announcement that we are each perfectly imperfect! Release the perfectionist and instead allow the Creative Genius within to be the source of your insights; open your heart to radiance, to what is blooming right now. In this field of *immeasurable* prospects, anything and all things are possible. Play with, explore, test, (and inevitably) accept this Truth and experience for yourself the liberty it delivers.

When we shift our awareness to our inner *wisdom*, to what lives beyond our thoughts, beyond our conditioning, and beyond our limiting beliefs, we find fulfillment through the remembrance of our Innate *wholeness*. And in doing so, we open and activate a much greater potential for the entire human family. We become available to more *glory*, more *joy*, more *love*, more *vitality*, more *prosperity*, more *creativity*, and more *peace* than we can currently imagine. We also show others how to do the same through our example.

To believe in something is not enough; to believe in Creative Genius or Infinite potential, or Divine Intelligence, is not enough to bring those qualities to the forefront of our experience. We need to participate through inspired action born of insight, also known as inner sight. We access our intuition, liberating our Inner Guidance System through practice. Devotion to one's own *conscious* unfolding yields great gifts, one of which is insight. Our perceptions change as we develop our meta-physical muscles. We gain understandings that we soon come to embody, for nothing feels better than the Truth. We are incarnations of Infinite Brilliance, and we have every right to walk this earth and act from an awareness of what we truly are. We are made in the "image and likeness" of the Creative Consciousness, a Love-Intelligence that knows no end to Its *expressivity*. It is our *inherent* right to shine as the *unique* embodiment of Cosmic Perfection expressed in physical form each one of us is. In surrendering to the Unknown, to the great mystery of Life, we unlock new levels of sacred Truth.

Scientific investigation demonstrates that active, intentional imagination and mental rehearing produce changes in brain structure. Someone intentionally envisioning themselves doing something produces the same brain circuits as someone doing that thing. Our thoughts create changes in our brains, while our emotions release chemicals in our bodies. Equipped with such *wisdom*, we find ourselves willing to become that which we wish to experience. We allow our Internal practice to feed us inspiration, and we listen to our Soul's *wisdom*. Our *Life* is a *unique* expression of *creative brilliance*, a celebration in acknowledgment of All There Is, the *great* Source of all Life Energy, this sanctified Universe, and all it contains. We are one with Creation, an undivided and essential part of All That Is, was, or ever will be.

We enquire within:

What is possible for my Existence?

How may I lovingly honor my Life?

What am I here to express?

What is emerging from within me?

"Nothing is meaningful except surrendering to love. Do it."

— RUMI

Worldly Challenges

"Art washes away from the soul the dust of everyday life."

— Pablo Picasso

Perspective

In the cocoon of her victimhood, my client dwelled in a place where shadows clung tightly to her, and every interaction became a battlefield. She bore the weight of past traumas like an indelible veneer, defining her existence and casting a somber hue over her perceptions of the world. Being near her was an emotional labyrinth, a journey through accusations and mistrust. The lens through which she viewed Life painted everyone as potential adversaries, and even the sincerest gestures of Love were met with skepticism.

Her trauma had become a narrative, a script she recited with unwavering conviction.

For years, attempts to break through this fortress of victimhood proved futile. The roots of her pain ran deep, and the identity she clung to seemed impenetrable. Love, kindness, and compassion were met with resistance as if any acceptance would be an abandonment of the familiar but suffocating comfort of blame and shame.

Then came a moment, a sliver in time that pierced through the dense clouds of victimhood. It was as though a switch had been flicked, and suddenly, she allowed herself to entertain the possibility that her beliefs weren't the sole *truth*. In that sacred moment of receptivity, transformation unfolded. As she relinquished the grip on her victim narrative, an alchemical change occurred. Her physiology responded to the newfound Light, and a radiant *vitality* replaced the heavy burden she had carried for almost her entire *Life*. Health, once held hostage, started to bloom. Laughter, buried beneath layers of limiting beliefs, erupted like a long-awaited Spring.

The stories of blame and shame began to unravel, revealing space for kindness, authenticity, and empowerment to flourish. Relationships, once strained by mistrust, became fertile grounds for joy and connection. Creativity, stifled by the weight of victimhood, surged forth in a cascade of inspiration. In the embrace of this transformation, she discovered the richness of a life not defined by past wounds.

The darkness that once veiled her perception lifted, and she basked in the warmth of newborn authenticity and originality. The journey from victimhood to empowerment was not easy, but the *beauty* that emerged from that transformation was nothing short of *magnificent*.

> "Whether you succeed or not is irrelevant; there is no such thing. Making your unknown known is the important thing."
>
> — GEORGIA O'KEEFFE

Life is not happening *to* you. You are happening *AS* Life. You co-create your experience, and perspective is an extremely useful tool to apply when in *conscious, intentional* collaboration with Creation. Through my experience making films and teaching filmmaking to actors and directors, I received a *beautiful* perspective I'd love to share with you. In the world of cinema, every frame helps tell the story, and filmmakers must learn the Art of Storytelling through the lens of a camera. One of the key elements I emphasized to aspiring filmmakers (both in front of and behind the camera) is the importance of camera angles and shot sizes in conveying emotions and non-verbal messages to the audience.

In cinematic communication, each camera angle and shot size has its own unique impact on the viewer. Terms like "close-up" (a frame size), "zoom in" (a camera movement), and "eye level" (a camera angle) are familiar to anyone in the industry, and they play a crucial role in capturing the essence of a scene. But it's not just about technicality; it's about applying these tools to evoke emotions and communicate ideas without words.

One of my favorite camera angles to explore was the "bird's eye view," also known as the high-angled "God P.O.V./Point Of View." Picture yourself soaring above, looking down on the scene below, or imagine observing yourself from a stable branch of a tall tree. From this perspective, you can perceive the characters and their surroundings with a sense of detached clarity. This angle could be considered a widened viewpoint that captures the big picture as opposed to minute detail.

What I find most fascinating about this angle is how it allows me to tap into my own sense of maternal Love for myself. It's a point of view, a sightline, that offers me the space to observe myself without judgment, to see my actions from a higher vantage point. It's a reminder that sometimes stepping back and up, facilitating a different perspective, can bring about a deeper understanding of myself and my experiences, as Life and as Art.

> *"A work of art which isn't based on feeling isn't art at all." ~*
>
> — Paul Cézanne

BELIEFS

The concept that thoughts are forms of energy compliments the metaphysical assertion that energy proceeds thought. Quantum mechanics validates this perspective with the theory that everything in the Universe is a Flow of Energy and that physical reality is fluid energy in Nature. It is said that we direct this Life-energy through our thinking and through our feelings. Known as Infinite Intelligence or Universal Consciousness, in some Spiritual circles, quantum mechanics refers to it as the "mental universe." It is said that Genius, expressed as extraordinary talents, is the manifestation of one's ability to commune with this Consciousness. Life Masters confirm that their exceptional skills stem from something beyond their comprehension. In other words, it is *ineffable* and beyond thought.

And yet, our mindset, our thoughts, our perceptions, and our beliefs are ever-present participants subconsciously contributing to our experience. Our micro-mental universe wants to guide our interpretations of our Life as we perceive it, believe it, and experience it to be. Perspective informs position, position informs points of view, and point of view informs opinion. We appear to bring to fruition not that which we think but rather that which we believe, unintentionally manifesting our fears more often than our wildest dreams. If we carry the deeply rooted and very human belief that we are not enough, that we are flawed, unlovable, and unworthy, we reap a Life of woe, loss, and loneliness. If we invest in the belief that "Life isn't fair," for example, a common adage parents and adults often tell children (and themselves) in an effort to protect, we will see and evaluate our experiences from that perspective, trapping our potential in a perpetual state of victimhood.

Thoughts and emotions are intimately connected: a thought is a form of mental energy with an emotional element attached, and an emotion is a form of mental energy with a cognitive element attached. Both are based in the past. They do not exist independently: thoughts generate emotion, and the essence of an emotion depends on the caliber of the thought. Intuition resides beyond our belief systems, beyond our social conditioning, beyond emotional content or thought. Before a thought, there is *light*, which is the spark of inspiration.

The personal perspective and interpretation of an event or experience is what causes the emotions around it. Our opinions, based on our positioning, create specific emotions which manifest into behavioral responses. Biological factors, belief systems, prejudices, and outlook all influence how we interpret Life. We call that our identity, and in doing so we interrupt our connection with our Inner Wisdom.

Practicing compassionate non-judgment and forgiveness towards all of Life inspires reconnection with our True Loving Nature.

"To change our state of being, we have to change how we think and feel."

— Dr. Joe Dispenza

Loving Affirmations

In exploring our inner self, we may come to understand that our self-love practice is lacking vitality and may be in need of some attention. For ease of use, perhaps the most accessible modality of practice is the personal affirmation. As an act of radical self-appreciation and celebration, we can construct self-supporting affirmative statements. With very little practice, affirming Life in a verbal manner soon becomes an easy and enjoyable talent.

Let's get started with a few phrases, with the intent of encouraging you to continue constructing your own. (Note: in parenthesis, following each declaration is an adapted version to be explored playfully should you experience an adverse reaction to speaking so affirmatively about yourself.)

- I love myself. I am a magnificent Being, whole, complete, and perfect, just as I am right now. *(It's as if I love myself. It's as if I am a magnificent Being; whole, complete, and perfect, just as I am right now.)*

- I am loved. I am worthy of love, I am lovable, and I am loving, always. *(It's as if I am loved. It's as if I am worthy of love, I am lovable, and I am loving, always.)*
- I am what I seek to be. What I seek is seeking me and is upon me. *(It's as if I am what I seek to be. As if what I seek is seeking me and is upon me.)*
- There is nothing I need to do or say or be in order to embody my greatness. I am great. Greatness is my Nature. *(It's as if there is nothing I need to do or say or be in order to embody my greatness. It's as if I am great. As if greatness is my nature.)*
- I am supported, surrounded by love, and always upheld by an Ever-Present Energy. *(It's as if I am supported, surrounded by love, and always upheld by an Ever-Present Energy.)*
- I allow Goodness to flow through me as me, as a Source of compassion and kindness toward all of Life. *(It's as if I allow Goodness to flow through me, as me, as a Source of compassion and kindness towards all of Life.)*
- I love fully and completely with no judgment or expectations of myself or others. *(It's as if I love fully and completely with no judgment or expectations on myself or others.)*
- I am one with all of Creation, with all living Beings, with the Earth and with the Universe. *(It's as if I am one with all of creation, with all living Beings, with the Earth, and with the Universe.)*

- I honor and serve the Highest Good within us all. I embody awareness as a choice. I gift myself the present moment over and over again, choosing creativity over self-doubt. *(It's as if I honor and serve the Highest Good within us all. As if I embody awareness as a choice. It is as if I gift myself the present moment over and over again, choosing creativity over self-doubt.)*
- I believe in Infinite potential as me. I am a beloved incarnation of Cosmic excellence. All is well. *(It's as if I believe in Infinite potential as me. It's as if I am a beloved incarnation of Cosmic excellence. It is as if all is well.)*
- I treat myself with love, and I am so grateful for the many ways I show myself love and appreciation. *(It's as if I treat myself with love, and it's as if I am so grateful for the many ways I show myself love and appreciation.)*
- Loving myself is my Inherent right. I gift myself forgiveness. I bow to the wisdom within me. *(It's as if loving myself is my Inherent right. It's as if I gift myself forgiveness. It is as if I bow to the wisdom within me.)*

Now, in the field of immeasurable possibilities, finish this phrase:

- I am willing to experience... *(It's as if I am willing to experience...)*

> "*Affirmations don't make something happen; they make something welcome.*"
>
> — MICHAEL BERNARD BECKWITH

EMOTION NOTIONS

Emotions are created by thought. We are not intellectual beings; we are Energetic Beings often stuck in emotionally reactive programs and patterns, as though we've been cast in a lifelong drama called "Retort." Emotion is past-based perception congestion lodged in the emotional body. Feelings are an Inner Guidance System, similar to a compass, incessantly tracking and informing us of our relationship with True Nature. Feelings, feeling tones, and vibrational realities, like notes being played on a mystical harp, are the gateway to higher thoughts, innovation, and creation. The thinking brain will label things as "good or bad" and "right or wrong" whereas the emotional brain will embody the thought, meanwhile the feeling aspect will simply vibrate as the thought. We experience our thoughts via our emotions.

I receive my most distracting invitations to behave without regard and from a place of justified insanity by the wannabe primary command center we all refer to as our emotions. Realizing that emotion is stuck energy that has the desire to move, transform, and then dissolve into the nothingness from whence it came, a gentle patience arises. Just like beloved children, my emotions are *magnificent* and *brilliant*, and are to be respected, looked after, and invited to sit in the back seat. My *Inner Wisdom* is driving this experience, not my gorgeously unpredictable HIGHLY REACTIVE emotional life, and every aspect of my Being is better off for that mature decision. My emotions are invited to come to play without judgment and, just as importantly, without any pressure to lead me. The simple act of bringing *loving* awareness to emotions creates the circuitry for the flow and movement of the trapped energy.

As I observe loved ones, be they clients, students, family, friends, or others, who invest strongly in the emotional aspect of themselves, I notice how their need to manufacture drama and false emotional highs and lows becomes evident as the addiction it truly is. Having to constantly produce emotions is an exhausting self-manipulation that harms its practitioner profoundly. I choose to opt for a more energy-effective reality and accept that emotional manipulation (over ourselves or others) is not within my highest field of affectivity. With respect and *loving* appreciation, I observe my emotions, and I *be* with them, *lovingly* and organically appropriating their level of influence over me.

"*You cannot heal what you do not feel.*"

— REV. DEBORAH JOHNSON

How wonderful to let my emotions be what they are without giving them the responsibility of interpreting All of Life, which is completely beyond their skill set, I understand. One of the beautiful aspects of practicing active awareness is that every action naturally births feeling tones or vibrations. I don't ever have to fake or produce energy as waves; they organically appear. Noting, again, that feelings express my current, present, Authentic Self, meanwhile, emotions report from the past. When I embrace that there is no proper or right emotion for any particular moment in Life, I liberate myself from the invention of any predetermined emotional state. With a developed skill for focusing my attention inwardly, as well as all around me, my *innate* feelings about whatever is transpiring become evident in a manner particular to that present moment. These feelings are present moment-based because they have no story attached to them; they are vibrational energies, often *ineffable*, though my emotional intelligence does love to try to name them!

In honor of my portable sanctuary, also known as my flesh and bone body, I've learned that feeling the emotion is the only way to move through the emotion and that avoiding emotions or focusing solely on them is what leads to illness. Denying my emotions is not the path to *freedom*. On the contrary, allowing myself to feel my emotions is self-liberation. Energy in motion is a *creative* tool: instead of avoiding my emotions, I get to put them to excellent use. E-motion is fuel for *creative* expression; the Vibrational Energy that I embody is what creates my experience.

An example of this arose several years ago during my last visit with my kidney specialist, which revealed that the progression of the previously diagnosed dis-ease within my organs had ceased. A scientifically predictable circumstance miraculously altered its expression, something my nephrologist has never seen in her almost forty-year career. The process wasn't linear, though I can describe it as specific choices I've made over the course of this particular healing journey.

Thanks to my established practice of meditation, breath work, sacred study, affirmative prayer, Intuitive movement, rest, and play, the diagnosis has shifted to a prognosis, and I can expect to live into "old age," whatever that means. I am grateful to declare the fullest expression of *wholeness* in, through, and as my body temple; thus, I gratefully decree that the Divinely orchestrated superb functioning of all organs and systems is mine to embody.

Besides making mindful choices for my physical well-being, such as important lifestyle changes, nutritional alterations, and bodily care practices, I consciously honored the deep-seated fear being housed in my organs, which I willingly listened to, profoundly felt as emotion, as I intentionally, compassionately forgave, and fully released them. It was a process that didn't happen overnight; although simple, it wasn't easy. I can testify to choosing my perspective and sustaining it relentlessly. My availability towards unknown possibilities certainly was key to allowing an Intelligence beyond my own to step in and have Its way with my body, mind, and Soul.

"Feeling is the secret."

— NEVILLE GODDARD

Feelings, which communicate through us, vibrating in and as our Sacred Instrument, cannot be manufactured. They must be tapped into like an underground river overflowing with resources, awaiting our awareness of it, so very ready to provide for us all of the insight, *wisdom*, and vision we can handle!

When, on the other hand, we strive for emotional results, suspended in a continual state of reaction, we discount so much of what we are. It forces us to assume one attitude or another, one opinion or another, which we believe we are obligated to recreate as part of our personality, which we feel we must somehow maintain and defend. That would be the precise moment we sacrifice the Truth for our vanity, disempowering along with it, our beloved Life Artist within. Our challenge becomes releasing our fear of the unknown and trading it for the Infinite possibilities packed in present-moment awareness.

If our attention is on manufacturing certain emotions, it certainly isn't focused on our highest intention. In moments like this, we find ourselves generalizing, making vast assumptions and assertions, and digging ourselves deeper into the pit of emotional justification proclamations. An indication that this may be happening is if we hear ourselves saying things mechanically. Another hint we may notice is if we find ourselves watching, judging, or criticizing what is going on in any memorized prefabricated way.

As I learned to embrace my own *unique* expression of Creative Genius, I got to become a space of authentic feeling, open and available to what is in any given moment. Knowing the Truth about my Inherent Creative Nature allows for a vast opening where everything that arises is honored, but not every thought nor every emotion is the boss of me. In the place of emotional roller coasters, a *prosperous*, overflowing inner garden burgeons where I get to play, *love*, express, and explore, unburdened by the muddy waters of old stories, old emotions, old identities.

> *"Creation is when the self is not there, because creation is not intellectual, is not of the mind, is not self-projected, is something beyond all experiencing, as we know it."*
>
> — J. Krishnamurti

The Myth of Personality

"Every act of creation begins with an act of destruction."

— Pablo Picasso

What if there were no such a thing as a personality? Who and what would I be?

If this contemplation stirs up a strong fear reaction, I immediately and compassionately understand the sensation is being brought to me by my *glorious* personality, the aspect of self that is frightful of extinction. And yet, for the sake of *creative* imagination and Spiritual *fun*, I invite myself to playfully ponder the release of the personality. I move through this contemplation gently so as not to incite my beloved ego into reaction.

This personality release occurs in Consciousness while involving no thought whatsoever. In its place, in the place of my personal identity, I notice there remains an Essence which aims to capture the multi-dimensionality of my particular Life experience.

If Life is Infinite, so am I; if the full spectrum of All That Is is within me, It is also within you. If that's the case, one's identity could be considered an illusion constructed for the ego's sake, as a form of protection from whatever it deems threatening, or as encouragement of anything it considers pleasing. Personality could have been conceived as a useful way of navigating Life on Earth, keeping the Being contained in something known and manageable, as opposed to admitting, accepting, and embracing that which the finite mind cannot comprehend. Given two options, which the binary intellect gladly provides, I suggest we go with the *affirmative*, *loving*, and more *beautiful* of the two.

But don't take my word on it. You know the Truth by the way it feels. So, ask yourself which is True: I am, and you are, finite creatures who are born and die and thus are limited to our bodies and the three dimensions within which we find ourselves currently, or I am, and you are *Immeasurably Creative Energetic Beings* Innately connected with and as an expression of *boundless* Life incessantly expanding in Its Consciousness as All That Is.

There is no separation; *wholeness* is a Universal Principle. Sentient Life is highly impressionable; if I emanate from a place of Wholeness, all of the Life forms around me will grant me the realization of that possibility. I am willing to understand, from moment to moment, what my Inner Wisdom is communicating through me, simultaneously allowing that intention to inform my actions. The Energetic Entity that is my Being acts out my mental images, and my actions are informed by my ideas of who and what I am.

As an Energetic Entity, stripped of personal identity, I notice that everything is vibrational. Peeling back the human costume, revealing the fluid light of different energetic frequencies, I am aware of the vibrational lifeforms affectionately known as *words*. Humans make sound, we invent words, and we invest powerfully in our words, endowing them with their own energetic vitality. We use words to define our lives, for they are the bricks with which we build the walls of our beliefs. We trust them, identify with them, and become them. And yet, words are superficial; they do not capture Life; they limit it. By naming a thing, our imagination about its possibilities becomes somehow locked in time and space. By identifying ourselves as one thing or another, we limit ourselves, locking our Essence in time and space. It is not right here to right now, but rather somewhere, someone in the past.

"Life is not about finding yourself. Life is about creating yourself."

— GEORGE BERNARD SHAW

Words create thoughts, create beliefs, create actions, and create reality. I declare, to name our Being anything other than *Infinitely Brilliant* seems to me a waste of words. Aristotle defined character as the sum total of an individual's actions, so *if* your personality exists, wouldn't it be possible to define it only as you take your last breath as "you"? The "sum total" does not imply a slice of, a percentage of, or a piece of; it means the Whole. And "actions" don't cease, so defining their total brings us back to where we began: Infinite unfolding possibilities within each physical manifestation of Life Energy. Gestures, manners, how we prefer our coffee or wear our hair, the trauma we've experienced, the food we've prepared, our opinions of current events, these things don't define us because they hardly serve our needs for compassionate connection and stronger relationships built on our Inner Genius. Feeling *fulfilled* and *whole* has no substitutes; therefore, we aren't even tempted to fall into the common traps of associating the superficial with the profound and mistaking the banal for the sublime. Possessing the clarity of mind to invest in a pure intention at any given moment is absolutely possible, regardless of how we dress, what language we speak, who raised us, what flavor of ice cream we love most, or any other external quality.

> *"Creativity is piercing the mundane to find the marvelous."*
>
> — BILL MOYERS

I become care-filled when I sense the impulse to reactively hide behind my stories, defending my "personality" as if it were at great risk. I can intuit fear and observe its root source where, with parental kindness, I uncover the ego in a state of panic, terrified and ready for a fight. The frightened, separated, isolated child cries, shouting at me, "I will NOT be put down!" and all at once, my entire Being, body, and surrounding energy field grows still and quiet. I whisper to my dear, precious ego that there will be no war today, that there is nothing to fear here, no one is being put down, and all is well.

In the primary stages of unfolding Consciousness, a healthy ego in the form of a *loving* sense of self is useful. I understand that there was a tendency to lean on the stories of being a type of person or having a type of character when I wanted to avoid discomfort or change. If I wasn't able to comprehend and accept the given circumstances (of the present moment) within which I could intuit my intentions based on my *innate Intelligence* and with respect for all forms of Life, and particularly for the ones with whom I chose to interact, no superficial mask, no character trait, no manners or gestures, were powerful enough to bridge those gaps. A fork in the road on my path of flourishing awareness became evident: all signs pointed to the realization that either I do the work to know and *Love* this experience for all that it is, or I do not. The choice was obvious, though not easy, not fear-free, not clean or tidy or neat. It was and continues to be *immense, undefinable, immeasurable,* and all that words cannot describe... although my intellect does love to try!

The ego sprouts up, sweetly participating, offering old repetitive contemplations: What was I supposed to be in order to be loved? Who was I when I felt approved of, included, connected, cherished, or seen? How was I behaving when someone, even myself, treated me with honor and respect? Which role must I inhabit, which tone must I speak with, and what must I exude so that I may experience kindness, humanity, and compassion? Ego isn't trying to upset or frighten me; it is offering up words for the sacrifice and the sacred releasing it is experiencing. More is available, I am aware; the space within, which is everywhere and nowhere, widens.

"Creativity takes courage"

— HENRI MATISSE

Love Constellation Game

This activity is one I invented for my own joyful maturation. One of my most critical personalities, and the one who inspired the creation of Love Constellation, is my old friend, "Madame Too So," who needed releasing as much as I needed to be liberated. In the process, I drew several portraits of her, let her write in my journal, and even let her speak unabashedly, aloud, and with my husband.

In Love Constellation, I invite you to embark on a heartwarming journey to release old aspects of yourself that no longer serve you. As you collect a constellation of personalities, your task is to shower them with Love until they dissolve, paving the way for your natural evolution.

How to Play:

Gather a group of friends, a single friend, or play solo. You may incorporate drawing paper, crayons or markers or paints, collages, and clippings if you have some old magazines/newspapers/illustrations handy or whatever excites you artistically. If you so choose, you can incorporate digital art as you please.

Each player imagines collecting one star from their private constellation of personality traits that represent different aspects of themselves.

Example: *I chose The Judge or the aspect of myself that is judgmental.*

- Visualize the personality trait chosen and breathe Life into it until it grows into a personality.
- Nobody knows your chosen personality trait better or more intimately than you; you know how it breathes, how it views the world and your place in

it, how it speaks, and what it says to you about you. A brief reflection on this personality trait will allow you to tap directly into the ways and manners of this aspect of your inner monologue.
- Draw what you observe.

Example: *I begin to see an elderly lady stooped over, and ornery. Elegantly dressed, she wears a hat and gloves and carries a cane and a heavy bag.*

- Write down the qualities, behaviors, perspectives, vocabulary, whatever occurs to you as ways to describe this personality.

Example: *Seeing her, I begin to notice how cruel she is to me! Given a voice (my attention) she is grumpy and furious, cursing and insulting me. She doesn't allow me any room for mistakes. She has an answer for everything. She seems to assume the worst about me.*

- Begin to embrace each personality with loving compassion and radical acceptance. If you are playing with others, this is the time to start sharing: tell your friend(s) about this personality. Give them a name.
- You may want to draw this personality trait, or write down some of their taglines, or cut out some letters and form a phrase with them.

Example*: I chose to "act it out," physically embodying my darling Madame Too So, giving her a voice and allowing her to be seen and heard. If that's too risky for you, go ahead and simply describe, illustrate, express, and embody, as best you can, this aspect of your personality you've chosen to release.*

- The gift of you dedicating conscious attention to this aspect of your personality breathes life into it, gives it a vitality that prevents it from alluding you or hiding from you. Notice that the more compassionate awareness you apply, as you allow it to be expressed, the less power it has. Note how your willingness to acknowledge and be with it, releases the severity of this old aspect that is seeking forgiveness. Let yourself appreciate this character, for they appeared to teach you something.
- As you shower each personality with forgiveness, appreciation, and Love, imagine them softening and dissolving into the Cosmic Energy around you.
- You can use affirmation, kind words, or gentle gestures (towards yourself), like resting a hand on your cheek or heart-center or caressing your arm, to express your Love as you share.

Example*: By allowing Madame Too So to fully express herself with my permission and absolute attention, I discovered her wicked sense of humor,* which I truly appreciate and have enjoyed over the years.

- Celebrate the release of each personality with joy and gratitude, knowing that it's an evolution towards your Higher Self.
- When you feel ready, take a moment to honor what this personality helped you with, recognizing that if it were present, it was at some point necessary for your survival. Realizing it is no longer necessary, express your gratitude to that aspect for all it contributed to your sense of safety.

Example: Madame Too So arose from within me to protect me; she wanted my skin to be thicker than it was; she judged me harshly based on my belief that I had to earn Love. I am so grateful for her sharp wit and biting language, for she never failed to capture my attention when my impulse to please would show up: she was a natural reaction to a behavior within me that denied my needs. Madame Too So did her best to protect me from my tendency to ignore myself! WOW! How blessed am I that she developed precisely when I needed her most! I am grateful.

- Continue until you feel lighter, freer, and wrapped in the warm embrace of Love, tenderness, acceptance, and compassion. Recognize that you are growing in Consciousness.

- Raise a cup of tea, a glass of juice, or whatever your preferred celebratory beverage may be in a toast to your old companion. Speak it out loud and with intention. Enjoy the salutation, for this is a goodbye.

Remember, the tone of the game is warm, playful, friendly, and fun. Approach it with a sense of curiosity, openness, and a willingness to explore the depths of your Being with Love and compassion. Enjoy the process of releasing old aspects and embracing the radiant Light of your True Nature!

"You don't need anyone else to love you to validate you. You are worthy because you are you, regardless of whether someone else loves you or not."

— BRADLEY NORTON

The reason why some individuals are so radiantly captivating in their uniqueness is that they've developed their skill for bringing their True Nature to the forefront of their Being, not just their intellect, not just their gut instincts, not just their Spirituality, not just their vast array of communicative talents, not just their compassion, not just their Inner Wisdom, but a wildly special combination of everything they embody and all they sense, in everything they do. This is the Art of Embracing Brilliance, and simply through our recognition of the possibility of It, we evolve. Right now, we get to admit that each one of us is a *unique* embodiment of Creative Genius seeking our Conscious awareness. And more, so much more!

Trusting my gifts and seeing my Divine identity, I am *free* to sparkle as only I can. Releasing my personal identity as a woman, daughter, artist, actor, practitioner, adopted child, wife, sister, and whatever other splintered versions of self that have arisen and been called by my name, I get a glimpse at my own *Infinitude* and multi-dimensionality. I am an *ineffable, boundless, unnamable, immeasurable Creation*, and so much more. And so are you. Eventually, even the term "Life Artist" may begin to feel restrictive as we remember our inherent unity with All That Is. I propose we keep it handy and play with it until it doesn't fit anymore, as a means of transmutation, transportation, and transformation.

Each of us, as a *unique* embodiment of the All of Life, is made to expand and flourish in ways that are exceptional and distinct to our individual expression of Life and in ways no one has ever seen or done before, dare we say, in ways none of us can currently imagine. We mustn't, nor can we, do as others have done before us, for no one is us. Instead, we remember that there is only one you and only one me, and although we are One, we each get to celebrate this Life in our own *unique* and exceptional way.

"God and Nature first made us what we are, and then out of our own created genius we make ourselves what we want to be. Follow always that great law. Let the sky and God be our limit and Eternity our measurement."

— MARCUS GARVEY

TEXT & SUBTEXT

Every art form has its Principles, fundamental, unchanging, and absolute Truths that act as the foundation for the medium's behaviors. An easy example of Principle is found in the fact that when anyone on Earth, be they a painter or not, mixes the color red with the color yellow, orange is the result. No matter one's age, ethnicity, politics, sexual preferences, gender identity, background, financial status, etc., the Law of Color stays the same. If that were not the case, it wouldn't be considered a Principle, a Law, or a Truth. Instead, it would be an opinion. Life Artistry has its own Principles, which are the same Laws that govern Nature. Life as Art has innumerable ways of expressing; because we are sharing this literature as a means of communication, let's explore a primary medium of Creation: Words.

Were my Life scribed in a screenplay or novel, in a court transcription or a poem, there would be the actual words on the page, and there would be any number of interpretations of those symbols brought forth by the impact of what is written and what is unwritten. What makes for great writing is the subtle *beloved* dance between what is said and what is unsaid: that which is nameable and that which is *ineffable*. This intimate relationship is one we've all enjoyed in our roles as audience members, readers, listeners, and observers of Life, as well as innate participants, communicators, co-creators, and Life Artists.

"The job of the artist is always to deepen the mystery."

— Francis Bacon

What we say matters: the words we select to define our experience influence our perceptions of Reality. Because we so closely identify with them, and we've charged them with values, words have energy; they have weight and vibration, and they are multi-layered. These are the three values of a spoken word: there is the Word itself, there is its delivery (how it is said), and then there is its intended impact (the intention behind it), each held by the speaker and each translated by the listener. When the speaker or the listener neglects their responsibilities, misinterpretation is highly likely.

The Principles of the Spoken Word

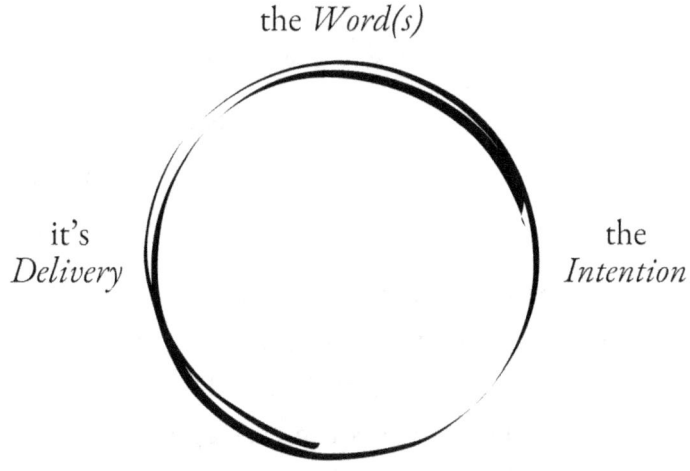

In exploring my response-abilities as a social Being, I acknowledge the difference between words, their delivery and their intention, well-aware that I'm not tied to any text or pre-written verbal score. In that recognition, I liberate my active Life Artist, inviting It to improvise with sincere *trust* in my awareness and skills for observation. When I am fully present in the moment, have accepted the given circumstances, have tapped into my Inner Guiding Wisdom, am permitting myself to act on my intentions in a flexible, full listening, receptive, responsive state, and allowing for the *fun* to unfold, I bring forth an *immeasurable* opening for revelations of possibilities, epiphanies, and discoveries. When I joyfully embrace responsibility for what I can actually affect, clarity in communication is highly probable. My ability to respond, also known as my "responsibility," is one of the greatest *creative* skills I have ever had the honor of honing.

> "If I could say it in words, there would be no reason to paint."
>
> — EDWARD HOPPER

It is our Inherent right and our function to bring ourselves to the fullest fruition possible, to a flowering as yet undefinable but real and palpable, nonetheless. We know it when we feel it. The more frequently and profoundly we feel it, the more real it becomes. If at any time we may worry whether or not we are doing this Life thing "correctly," we create a moment of reflection for ourselves where we can remember forgiveness and total acceptance. We've released the habit of judging ourselves.

> "If I create from the heart, nearly everything works; if from the head, almost nothing."
>
> — MARC CHAGALL

Accepting the Calling

"What moves men of genius, or rather what inspires their work, is not new ideas, but their obsession with the idea that what has already been said is still not enough."

— Eugene Delacroix

We each have a calling on our Life; each one of us has been called forth, beckoned, and summoned to awaken to the presence of Creative Genius within. *Inseparable, Indivisible Wholeness* is an aspect of the Cosmos, and everything I know as Life is interconnected. As an individual member of this thing called Life, I am part of a much Grander Whole. An awareness of this Truth gained through sacred study and deep Spiritual contemplation, is important for me to cultivate. My intellect wants its part, so I read the latest scientific theories and discoveries available; just as my heart wants its part, thus, I become a space in Consciousness where physical and metaphysical unite and synchronize.

When my gut, my heart, and my brain are in collaborative alignment, *harmony* cannot help but exude from my very Being, my Life, and my affairs. My relationship with my Authentic Being, with my True Nature, offers me an Infinitude of opportunities for forgiveness, compassion, kindness, friendship, *joy*, *love*, understanding, *freedom*, *creativity*, and so much more. Each Now-moment of my Life is a new, wonderful occasion of unfoldment and blossoming. My Existence is the greatest gift the Spirit of the Universe could give me, and awareness is my greatest tool. Here and now, I choose to allow and accept all that is revealing itself to me, though me, as me. I accept the call to Greatness. I invite you to join me.

> *"We are one. Only egos, beliefs, and fears separate us."*
>
> — NIKOLA TESLA

Human connection through interaction is one of the most important skills I, as a Social Spiritual Being, can care to develop. Each relationship I choose to cultivate offers new and unexpected variables, including individual perspectives, beliefs, versions of reality, opinions, fears, reactions, and habits. Each individual has their own approach to experiencing Life and Love. Though suffering is often essential for awakening something larger within, it is not a productive state from which to create because it is not my True Essence, and thus, tends to bring to fruition only more pain. Instead, I treat myself to a few righteous revelations that can uphold the structures of my Being.

I get to be kind to myself; I get to gift myself with the recognition of *peace, fulfillment, Love*... everything I know to be Universal Principle, everything I know as my Soul's desire, everything my Authentic Self wants to experience as me, in this incarnation. Practicing the Art of Awareness delivers an invitation to recognize the living Law of Allowance, which is experienced through and as me. It is a choice and a gift for the Life Artist who courageously agrees to co-create with the medium of Consciousness. We are doing it all the time anyway; we might as well intentionally allow it and enjoy it.

Self Advocacy

Continuing to nourish our immeasurable creativity as Life Artists, we get to make declarations that support our True Essence. Below are a few statements you can read aloud each morning while looking in the mirror. You may find yourself, especially when just beginning mirror-work, uncomfortable, uneasy, and seeking an escape from the opinions that arise while speaking these reflections. Stick with it, and within a day or two, notice a shift in not only your comfort levels but in your playful willingness to make such loving proclamations. Soon thereafter, your Creative Genius will join the fun, and you'll find yourself ready to speak your own words in your own unique way.

Say out loud as you look into your own eyes:

I release old habits and patterns, granting more space for my willingness to listen, receive, and allow.

I embody peace within through forgiveness for all that was, all that is, and all that will be.

I am mindful of my Social-Spiritual need for real connection, and when someone trusts me, myself included, I am worthy of that faith.

I nurture compassion as I communicate my intentions with gentle awareness and expanded intelligence, never with force or violence.

I maintain childlike flexibility in my thoughts, beliefs, behaviors, actions, and words, for none is useful once set in stone.

I surrender fully to my Innate Goodness, trusting that Life is indeed for me and never against me.

I love courageously, ever radiating from my heart-center my connectedness with All There Is.

Founding my practice on merits such as these elevates me above small-mindedness, opinions, and other unsettling disturbances common in daily unconscious living. My intuition informs me of which situations and states to disregard or allow. I release my attachment to dualism and opposition. And I affirm, the ideal way to rid my Life of profound suffering is through mindfulness, heart-fullness, union with Source, and intentional action. I am comfortable with not knowing and not having to know; I have become dear friends with The Unknown and embrace it as fully as I would a cherished loved one.

My heart, my Inner Wisdom and the Life-Energy that I am made of, these are my guides. I work for them and answer only to them, for they have the final say on all I endeavor to create, express, or realize. I sense I am here with purpose; I am aware of what my responsibilities entail, and I acknowledge All of Life with reverence.

Judgment and condemnation no longer reside within me. Instead, I choose to question gently, to explore, and, with endless curiosity, to offer myself in service of a Higher Good. With ease and permission, I allow what is to reveal itself to me. I need not beseech or beg, I need not seek; I am perfectly *whole*, and all of my needs are met right here and right now. All is well. Disrespect and disorder are not Universal Principles. Therefore, they are not an organic part of me. I put chaos to sleep with a lullaby of natural *order*, *balance*, and *harmony*, letting radical *joy* take the place of stagnate fear.

What feels like suffering within can only appear when I am role-playing, forcing, comparing, ignoring, or nursing any other behaviors or vibrations that ignore my Greatest Good. I ask that an internal alarm sound should I ever find myself compromising what I instinctively sense to be True about All of Life, if I am in danger of betraying my Authentic Self, when I forget what and who I am, permitting experiences of humiliation, violation, inhumanity.

> *"Authentic human interactions become impossible when you lose yourself in a role."*
>
> — Eckhart Tolle

There is no rehearsal; this is the main event and is always/only happening right now. I have a choice, in every single moment, of which vibrations I wish to feel, transmit, exchange, and embody. For the Love of *fun* and *Infinite possibility*, I suggest we "go big," as it is said. And yes, I know the Life Artist in each one of us can feel what "going big" means in our individual lives. Whatever sparks your Joy for Living is a necessary, unnegotiable variable in your personal *peace* equation.

When I share my visions and inspirations with others, it requires a heightened ability to listen, observe, and honor without judgment. Recognizing that everyone carries their unique struggles and challenges, just as I do, emphasizes the importance of accepting others and myself just as we are. We all grapple with habits, beliefs, and behaviors that may grip us tightly, and sometimes, a simple act of acceptance can open hearts. My vocation is not to heal others or myself but to embody my Innate *wholeness* and operate from a place of *balance*. Engaging fully with others can be a profound teacher, offering lessons yet undiscovered.

In the grand scheme of things, no thought, even the cranky, clueless, or frightened ones, is a real troublemaker, at least not initially. The potential for risk kicks in when those thoughts ignite vibes (also known as feelings) that then take a stroll into action. It's not about the wild ideas I entertain but how I jive with them energetically, in my personal frequency reverberation, as I dance with the Cosmos. Good or bad thoughts? Nah, not my jam, even though I can observe high-flying, positive groove thoughts and low, dense, not-so-fun, not fully truthful ones. Luckily, the steering wheel for thoughts and actions is in my hands, and I'm cruising in the heart lane, guided by my ever-expanding inner smarts and the Universal Principles I've got on speed dial.

> *"The most common form of despair is not being who you are."*
>
> — KIERKEGAARD

When a wave of rage, aggression, or pain tries to crash the party, I don't have to act upon it because I am grounded in my craft, aware that such vibrations can be real buzzkills for my imagination and creativity. I feel it, I allow it, and I keep it moving in honor of the Life Force flowing, always moving through me and through Everything That Is. Experiencing interconnection with myself through inner communion and expression is possible, even when emotions throw a little tantrum. Sure, there may be resistance present, but that doesn't mean I'm joining the brawl. In my willingness to simply be with that seeming polarization, conflict, or resistance, I am allowing something new to occur. I let myself *be*, without attachment to any ideal.

I've kicked the habit of carrying the heavy baggage of yesteryears around with me, coloring my experience, twisting every day into a rerun of misery. I no longer allow such falsity to invade my relationships or conversations. I'm all about *loving* in the present moment, letting Life unfold like a surprise gift, and seeing *beauty* in every nook and cranny of Existence. Even when I perceive only darkness, yes, even when I am on my knees, I get to remember something greater than my perceptions is occurring. I get to learn how to sit with myself lovingly.

I intend to carry very little with me as I learn to leave that which no longer serves behind, shedding the weight of untruthful old habits. Thus, I get to be energetically and intentionally light, supple, flexible, and ready, come what may. As I deepen my relationship with all that Source is, I fortify my greatest connection with my Truest Self, one of the coolest repercussions of which is it opens my heart to authenticity, intimacy, vulnerability, closeness, and exchange, organically encouraging others to do the same. It is a Love ripple effect.

Life is a Cosmic Living Masterpiece, within which I am morphing, adapting, and adjusting on the fly and in sync with my Highest, Greatest Good. Sure, I might encounter lower vibrational Lifeforms now and then, but they are way fewer than the compassionate, awakened, heart-led, high-vibrating crew I choose to collaborate with while on Earth. When I'm in the company of bottom-feeders or energy vampires, I've got a palette full of choices to apply. My craft is to embody all that I am in any given moment, which may or may not involve dialogue or interaction.

The Universe is indeed friendly, and thus, so shall I admit and commit to being. I was born *pure, complete, good*, loved, and oh-so-wanted. I'm no longer playing hide-n-seek with my True Nature; It is here, within me, summoned, basking in *Love* and *Light*, and ready for continued co-creative *brilliance*.

> *"Once you make a decision, the universe conspires to make it happen."*
>
> — Ralph Waldo Emerson

Spark Joy Practice

Take a moment to sit comfortably and gently lower your gaze.

Breathe slowly, intentionally inhaling positive Intelligence (energy that is charged with positivity) and intentionally exhaling any tension or old negative residue.

Now, visualize a radiant spark of joy within your heart-center. Picture it as a vibrant, glowing light. Perhaps it is radiating a certain color you find joyful.

With each breath, allow this spark to expand... until it grows into a blazing flame that permeates your entire Being.

Feel the warmth and vitality exuding outward, enveloping you in a cocoon of pure joy.

As you continue to breathe, release any residual negativity or stress, let the resistance go, see it burn up and disappear, and notice your flame growing brighter.

Picture yourself surrounded by the people, places, and things that bring you immense joy and fulfillment. Allow your flame to expand and embrace all that you love and cherish.

Remain in this joy-filled space for as long as you wish, soaking in the positivity.

When you lift your gaze, choose to embody this radiant joy for the rest of your day.

Notice how your Internal Light ignites the spark of joy in others, kindling a wave of immeasurable positivity in the world.

Cosmic Director

I find incredible *beauty* in celebrating the awareness that all things are working together for my Highest Good, *beauty* in my willingness to recognize that all of my experiences are defined by my positioning in the immeasurable Intelligence of Creation, and *beauty* in the awareness that *wholeness* is an Innate aspect of Life. Steeped in this *wisdom*, I declare I am the animator of all the perspectives in my story... thus arriving at an empowering application of my abilities.

> *"I have to act to live."*
>
> — Sir Lawrence Olivier

With all of this newly nourished artistry bubbling over, let's circle around to revisit our previous pretend night-at-the-theater event and the varying perspectives we explored in our fictitious production way back when we began this adventure together. With playful and empowered curiosity, let's return once more to that imaginary circumstance. This time, however, let's go beyond imagining; let's embody it!

Feel into these possibilities. You are your own Artistic Director; your individual active intention is being brought to *light*, and the play itself is your very Life. There is no role to play. Instead, you get to just *be*, which is so much more than enough. Bear witness to what is emerging from within, for you are the Creative Consciousness through which Source is expressing.

All of Life, this entire production, has been created with your Highest Good at heart and, through your willingness, is being brought to fruition. All That Is is in service of the Creative Genius that you are. You now have the honor of being this opus's eyes and ears, for it is through your senses and sensibilities, through your awareness and willingness, that this Masterpiece will find fulfillment. As a unique emanation of *immeasurable Brilliance*, what you perceive and how you receive influences your *creative* capacity. Your vibration, your heartbeat, your central nervous system, your energy field, and your essence set the tone for your experience.

Choose well, aim high, go deep.

> "The key to growth is the production of higher dimensions of consciousness into our awareness."
>
> — Lao Tzu

All of Nature will serve your vision of Life. Everything That Is will conspire to provide what you are willing to allow for yourself from within. You are and always have been an effortless, *creative* collaborator. You are crafting the Life you came here to participate in from a place of *wholeness* and worthiness; you've got all the necessary skills, and you've got the support of the Universe behind you.

Audience = You (your Authentic Self), which is inseparable from Divine Consciousness.

Writer = Your Authentic Self that has a mind temple.

Actor = Your Authentic Self that has a body temple.

The theater = Wherever you are.

The play's title = "Heaven on Earth."

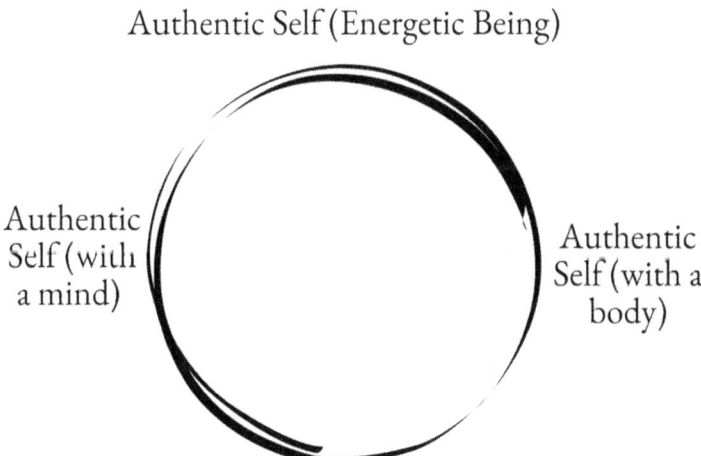

"We came here to create heaven on earth."

— Dr. Bruce Lipton

Invite and allow this as your Reality. Admit how capable you Truly are and acknowledge how free you are when you allow your True Essence to inform your Life story.

"The secret of change is to focus all of your energy, not on fighting the old, but on building the new."

— Socrates

Embracing It All

"Life is your art. An open, aware heart is your camera. A oneness with your world is your film. Your bright eyes, your easy smile is your museum."

— Ansel Adams

With playfulness and practice, with Luminosity and Love, with intentionality and willingness, our Inner Life Artist finds a welcoming core, heart, and mind to nurture It into Its fullest, *limitless* expression. As an organically intuitive embodiment of Love manifesting the contents of your *glorious* Consciousness, may you recognize your *awesomeness* now and in every passing moment. Expressing all that you are as truthfully as possible occurs only in the moment where your active presence exists.

"In art, what we want is the certainty that one spark of original genius shall not be extinguished."

— Mary Cassatt

The natural talents associated with being a Creative Genius (i.e., compassion, sensitivity, high awareness, sensuality, vulnerability, artistry, insight, inspiration, ability, authenticity, expression, etc.) are all already a wholesome integral part of who you are; every human being is born Brilliant, you included. What makes an individual shine brightly in the midst of creating is our availability to respond based on what our True Nature reveals. May you experience the overflowing abundance of possibilities that self-knowingness, with Love, joy, and gratitude, provides.

When we fall back on habitual behaviors, we play the fool and end up with no talent for Life. Instead, we become a predictable series of memorized reactions rooted in fear. We manifest misery for ourselves and others, but we call it "my" truth, forcing ourselves to identify with something not actually Truthful or occurring right now. How great is the self-honor and *wisdom* of the Being that can call upon their highest self, tapping into Universal Law at any given moment and within any given circumstance, thanks to an expanded, dedicated practice nurtured with Love, care, and kindness, which can see us through even the most overwhelming of experiences!

In every moment, you have an opportunity to consciously develop your own reliable and personal set of Life-Artistry skills. No matter who you interact with, no matter where you may find yourself putting your Genius to use, you will have the ability to put valuable and worthwhile energy in motion, to take a stand for connection, intimacy, growth, courage, compassion, to proclaim your greatest intentions, and then to be exactly what you came here to be; thus, creating a world more *beautiful* than any one of us can currently imagine or has ever known.

May you be liberated and empowered to take action from a place of *peace*-filled *enthusiasm*. May you notice that you have the *power* to move the masses, to accompany the species on the path of *enlightenment*, to inspire awareness, courage, compassion, forgiveness, positivity, and playfulness simply through your willingness to respond to what you observe within. Nothing is more joyful, more thrilling, or more inspiring than witnessing another Being stand in their True Essence, loyal to their Soul's intentions, come what may.

Just as all of Nature is in full expression of Itself, so does Life expect you to be! Your very *life* is a Masterpiece; you are the purpose of your existence. The *creative expression* that you naturally embody is already *perfect*, and you were designed for Its full emergence as you. Your every word, thought, and action is your Sacred palette with which you are *free* to express. *Consciousness* creates. And we all get to be empowered participants in the creation of the world we'd love to live in. Glory is more than a birthright; it is an *Innate*,

Inherent, and *Omnipresent* variable in the equation called "self." Self-expression without real self-awareness is egoic self-centered service. Whereas, when self-awareness precedes self-expression, it brings to fruition Creative Genius AS individualized self.

The contents of this book will not make you what you already are, the embodiment of Cosmic Brilliance. It is merely a drop in the bucket of your collected resources. Use the information you find valuable, and toss the rest aside, for it is your *inherent* right to craft your own personal approach to this *glorious* awakening called Life. Invent and uncover ways to practice what you've found applicable. Be kind and patient with your Inner Innate Genius, be *loving*, be ideal, have a sense of humor, and have *fun*.

> *"Creativity is intelligence having fun."*
>
> — Albert Einstein

As we willingly invest in our individual expansion by honoring our intuition, respectfully nurturing our devotional practice, and living and moving with great intention, all of the skills we develop strengthen. Our Being upgrades energetically, able to sustain more *Luminosity*, more *Brilliance*, and more *Possibilities*.

If the thought of living Life in the unknown present moment, *free* of all that the past and future would have us grasping at in blindness, sets our hearts to racing, sparking a smile, excitement, or *enthusiasm* within, it is clear: we will contribute to the conscious evolutionary transformation already in progress. We are eternally *united* in service of the *Creative Genius*, all forms of Life, and the Earth itself in a *powerful*, important, *loving* way that only each one of us can embody.

"To create one's own world takes courage."

— GEORGIA O'KEEFFE

My Sincerest Gratitude

> *"The more I think it over, the more I feel that there is nothing more truly artistic than to love people."*
>
> — Vincent Van Gogh

As this manuscript came into fruition, you were ever in my heart. Finally, I get to express my thanks to you directly, Dear Life Artist. I am so grateful you're reading these words, for that must mean we've traveled briefly together as you journeyed through these writings. Thank you for walking with me as I *Embrace Brilliance* as the Inherent blessing, and Truth of my Being, it is. Your curiosity and playful willingness are greatly appreciated by me as I continue to celebrate our Innate Creative Genius.

This book would not have been possible without the support of my beloved family and friends. My inner "talkative" child has matured into a wordsmith because of your patience and nurturing. In particular, I would love to acknowledge the following people for their support, guidance, and wisdom: Asli Eti, Deborah Varn, Michael Gast, Kevin Pratt, Carol & Jack Dulske, Marge Tessier, Paola Castro, Merredith Brittain, Daniel Parizek, Graham Steele, Aida Zorilla, Courtney Reeve, Daniel Roquéo, Eileen Norton, Frank Norton, Constance Norton, Christopher & Roni Norton, Bradley Norton, Elisabetta Ballerini, Marco & Marta Ballerini, Jayne Elizabeth Gall Carilo, Kevin Pratt, Michael Gast and my darling Dante.

A sacred nod to the entire Agape International Spiritual Center and the Practitioner Core; I am forever grateful to Dr. Rev. Michael Beckwith, Rev. Cheryl Ward, Rev. Coco Stewart, Rev. Susan Shahani, Rev. Kim Stanwood Terranova, Mitch Earle, Matthew Baumeuller, Rev. Cynthia Ambriz, Rev. Jason D. Mitchell, Julie Giordano, Rev. Carlton Teabout, Eisha Mason, Ama Mystic, Rev. Kathleen McNamara, Jerrilynne Bossett, Leigh Brown, Jacquelyn Brown, Jennifer Capler, Rev. Deborah Johnson, and the Love Ninja tribe.

My most enthusiastic gratitude goes to my publishers at *The Good House*, in particular, Karen Alston-Mills and Sean Patrick; thank you for creating and sustaining a safe, joyous space that upheld and encouraged the author within to flourish as this manuscript wrote itself through me. My gratitude for you both is immeasurable.

A special acknowledgment must be given to my husband, Mario "Baba" Castegnaro, for his ongoing patience, his Innate kindness, and his incessant loving care, for which I am eternally grateful. Thank you for embodying Home for me.

I love you.

Bibliography

Aristotle: *Metaphysics*
Aurelius, Marcus: *Meditations*
Beckwith, Michael Bernard: *Life Visioning*, *The Answer is You*, and *Spiritual Liberation*
Brown, Brenè: *The Power of Vulnerability*
Bruder, Melissa; Cohn, Lee Michael; Olnek, Madeleine; Pollack, Nathaniel; Previto, Robert; and Zigler, Scott: *A Practical Handbook for the Actor*
Campbell, Joseph: *The Power of Myth*
Chödrön, Pema: *When Things Fall Apart: Heart Advice for Difficult Times*
Coelho, Paulo: *The Alchemist*
Cutler, Howard: *The Art of Happiness: A Handbook for Living*
Dispenza, Joe: *Becoming Supernatural*
Dooley, Mike: *Infinite Possibilities*
Dwyer, Wayne: *The Power of Intention*, and *Change your Thoughts, Change your Life*
Eckhart, Meister Johannes: *Selected Writings* and *The Complete Works*
Emerson, Ralph Waldo: *The Complete Essays & Other Writings*
Gandhi, Mahatma Mohandas K.: *The Essential Gandhi: An Anthology of His Writings on His Life, Work, and Ideas*
Goddard, Neville: *The Power of Awareness*
Goldsmith, Joel: *The Infinite Way*, and *The Art of Spiritual Healing*
Haase, Cathy: *Acting for Film*
Hawkins, David R.: *The Eye of the I*, and *Discovery of the Presence of God*
Hesse, Herman: *Siddhartha*
Holmes, Ernest: *The Science of Mind*, *This Thing Called You*, and *Creative Mind*
Krishnamurti, Jiddu: *On Love*, *Think on These Things*, and *Freedom From the Known*
Lipton, Bruce H.: *Biology of Belief*
Luna, Aletheia: *Awakened Empath: The Ultimate Guide to Emotional, Psychological and Spiritual Healing*

Morter, Sue: *The Energy Codes*
Northrup, Christine: *Making Life Easy*
Osho: *Vigyan Bhairav Tantra*, and *love, freedom, aloneness: The Koan of Relationship*
Plato: *Symposium*
Pressfield, Steven: *The War of Art*
Rinpoche, Sogyal: *The Tibetan Book of Living and Dying*
Shinn, Florence Scovel: *The Power of the Spoken Word, The Game of Life and How to Play It; The Secret Door to Success,* and *Your Word is Your Wand*
Stanislavski, Konstantin: *My Life in Art*
Terranova, Kim Stanwood: *The Technology of Intention*
Thurman, Howard: *The Inward Journey,* and *The Sound of the Genuine*
Tolle, Eckhart: *The Power of Now* and *A New Earth: Awakening to Your Life's Purpose* and *A Dialogue with Ram Dass*
Tzu, Lao: *Tao de Ching*
Williamson, Marianne: *A Return to Love*

About the Author

Jennifer Norton is a radiant force, bridging spirituality and fine arts to empower global transformation. Her practices, a fusion of metaphysics, sacred wisdoms, and creativity, unfold as a testament to compassion, self-liberation, and Soulful Self-realization. As a certified life coach, meditation guide, mindfulness mentor, and Agape Licensed Spiritual Practitioner, she guides seekers toward Soul expression, celebrating each life as a masterpiece waiting to be unveiled.

Infusing joy and reverence into her approach, Jennifer empowers Life Artists to unlock their creative genius and *embrace* their *brilliance*. With warmth and authenticity, she facilitates hallowed spaces for Spiritual growth, drawing from her intuitive, clairsentient nature and extensive experience as a self-healer and mystic. A world traveler and Gaian, Jennifer's 35+ relocations enrich her connection to humanity's collective journey. Fluent in English and Italian, she extends her impact through speaking engagements, educational programs, and creative ventures, embodying the boundless potential of conscious living. Through her offerings and guidance, Jennifer invites individuals to reclaim their inherent creativity, unlocking the full spectrum of their potential. Jennifer Norton illuminates the path to authentic expression, inviting all to embrace their divine essence and co-create a world filled with love and purpose.

To know more, please visit:

www.jennorton.com

www.facebook.com/iamjennorton

www.instagram.com/iamjennorton